SCHOLARS

and

MYSTICS

Sister Mary Jeremy, O.P.

HENRY REGNERY COMPANY
Chicago 1962

To the happy memory of the saints of Helfta
GERTRUDE THE GREAT AND MECHTILD
—and of J.B.F. who knows them now.

Nihil Obstat: V. Rev. Patrick M. J. Clancy, O.P.,
   Censor Deputatus.

Imprimatur: Albert Cardinal Meyer, S.T.D., S.S.L.,
   Archiepiscopus Chicagiensis, January 15, 1962.

Foreword

The only woman in Germany called "the Great," St. Gertrude of Helfta is at once known and unknown. Many churches are dedicated to her; she is quoted in books on mysticism; her role in the development of the devotion to the Sacred Heart is acknowledged. Besides these perennial reminders of the saint, there are some references to her in unlikely places: Mauriac, writing in the *Saturday Evening Post* series, "Adventures of the Mind," quotes from her *Exercises;* Maritain in his correspondence with Jean Cocteau writes, "St. Gertrude wanted to recover all love for Jesus," and then adds a long passage from her *Legatus;* two German scholars, H. Grössler and W. Preger, insist that the saint was really a pre-Reformation Protestant, basing their argument chiefly on her devoted study of the Scriptures. As Ledos, her French biographer observes, their efforts to claim her for themselves "are a tribute to the attraction exerted by her angelic spirit."

The general impression of the life and work of St. Gertrude is, nevertheless, somewhat vague. Most of the scholarship on the saint is in Latin, German, or French and has not been utilized by English writers. (An exception is the Benedictine nun of Regina Laudis who has recently issued an excellent edition of the *Exercises* of St. Gertrude.) Even in books published within the past ten years the saint is confused with her abbess, Gertrude von Hackeborn, although this error was exposed by the Solesmes Benedictines more than eighty years ago.

In the following pages I have tried to relate the saint's visions to her personality, her environment, and her apostolate. The familiar title of the nineteenth-century English translation, *Revelations of St. Gertrude,* (which was not the original designation of her *Legatus*) may lead some readers to give undue importance to her presentation of the spiritual through the sensory. Clearly she herself was free from that taste for the marvelous which, as Père Régamey affirms, is harmful to pure faith. Her vivid images have a beauty of their own; their effect is a strengthening of faith and devotion. Dom John Chapman has said, "St. Gertrude impresses us with the vastness of her theological horizon, in spite of the pictorial nature of her conceptions."

The only source for the saint's biography is the *Legatus Divinae Pietatis,* written in part by herself and in part by an anonymous "compilatrix" who lived in the same convent. The authenticity of this work has never been questioned.

The definitive Solesmes edition of *Legatus,* supplemented by the French translations, has been my chief authority. My aim has been not to write a biography of St. Gertrude, but to present some aspects of her personality, her writings, her intellectual interests, her spirituality, and the convent where she lived from the age of five until her death some forty years later.

As Jean Leclercq has observed, hagiographical legends are "an important and too little exploited source of information on the customs and ideals in the monastic milieu." From the *Legatus* and its companion volume, the *Liber Specialis Gratiae,* which treats of St. Mechtild, the friend and confidant of St. Gertrude, emerges a composite picture not only of the two saints but also of the remarkable community of which they were active and influential members. Under the leadership of an extraordinary abbess these women made thirteenth-century Helfta a place where high spirituality was combined with intellectual and manual labor. Most of the nuns were aristocrats while St. Gertrude was a nameless orphan, but diversity of background and personality proved no obstacle to the ardent charity uniting the community during one of the stormiest periods of German history.

The few external events in Gertrude's life are not set forth chronologically in the *Legatus*. The discursive style of the saint and her collaborator has created problems in organization. In trying to solve them I have been unable to avoid some repetition and arbitrary placing of various incidents. For my apology I borrow St. Joseph's words from Lydgate's *Lyf of Our Lady:*

Have me excusid of my derke dulnesse. . . .

Till for her God list better to provyde.

The association of the saint and her community with members of the order of Preachers is well attested. To add one link to the chain which unites the children of St. Dominic to "this royal soul" is an enduring privilege.

For helpful information concerning the present state of the buildings in Eisleben-Helfta I am grateful to Monsignor Gerhard Fittkau of Essen-Werden. I wish to acknowledge the permission granted by Longmans, Green, and Company to quote from Lucy Menzies' *The Revelations of Mechthild of Magdeburg.*

Epiphany, 1962

SISTER MARY JEREMY, O.P.
Rosary College
River Forest, Illinois

Table of Contents

 *The Book of Helfta*

HISTORICAL RÉSUMÉ

Date	Site	Abbesses
1229	Mansfeld Foundation	Cunegunde v. Halberstadt
1234	Rodardsdorf	Cunegunde v. Halberstadt
		Gertrude v. Hackeborn
		(not St. Gertrude)
1257	HELFTA	
	The Three Mystics:	Gertrude v. Hackeborn
	Mechtild v. Magdeburg	
	(ex-beguine)	
	St. Mechtild	
	(sister of Abbess)	
	St. Gertrude	Sophia v. Mansfeld
		Jutta v. Halberstadt
		Sophia v. Friedburg
1346	Eisleben	Luitgard v. Mansfeld

Helfta

The monastery of St. Mary at Helfta was at once representative and outstanding among the conventual establishments of 13th-century Saxony. Called "the crown of German cloisters" and set in a place of great natural beauty, it was not only a center of culture, both literary and artistic, but a school of solid spirituality as well.

During its flowering time, three of the Church's greatest mystics lived at Helfta as members of this religious community: St. Gertrude the Great, her friend St. Mechtild von Hackeborn, and the ex-beguine Mechtild von Magdeburg.

Founded in the year 1229 within the castle precincts of Mansfeld and later moved to Rodardsdorf, the community had finally settled at Helfta where it was to acquire its reputation for learning and culture. This period of renown began in 1251 with the election of the Abbess Gertrude von Hackeborn, and ended in approximately 1302 with the death of her namesake, St. Gertrude the Great, the last and most famous of the convent's three great mystics.

The subsequent history of the community is a troubled one. The invasion of Helfta by Albert of Brunswig in 1342 brought about another change in location and the community was transferred to Eisleben or "new" Helfta.

Since 1959, the ruins of the convent church at "old"

Helfta have been protected as an historical monument. With the rest of Thuringia and East Saxony, however, both "old" and "new" Helfta are now under Communist domination.

GARDEN AND BATTLEFIELD

From its earliest beginnings, the community at Helfta was distinguished by the religious fervor of its lay benefactors as well as of its members. Two anecdotes illustrate the personal holiness of its founders, Elizabeth of Schwartzburg, and her husband, Burchard, Count of Mansfeld.

On one occasion, after the death of her husband, the countess went on a pilgrimage to Marpurg to visit the tomb of her patroness, St. Elizabeth of Hungary. Among the throngs crowding at the grave was a poor man carrying an afflicted child who apparently had been born without eyes. Not knowing who the countess was, he asked her to carry the baby up to the saint's grave. Overcome with pity, Elizabeth took the little one in her arms and prayed fervently that God would show his mercy through the intercession of St. Elizabeth, thinking as she did so, that she herself was wholly unworthy of obtaining such a favor. She meditated penitently on the contrast between the saint's life and her own, reproaching herself especially for having used her eyes to enjoy frivolous and worldly sights. Nevertheless, despite her conviction of guilt, she prayed with confidence that God would give sight to the infant she was holding. Suddenly the Countess heard a crackling sound "as of parchment tearing" and, to her amazement, saw that the skin covering the place of the eyes had opened, revealing bright grey eyes, while the child wailed loudly and all the bystanders were filled with wonder.

Until the end of her life, the old account concludes, this child born blind had perfect vision. One can well imagine that the story, told and retold at Helfta, caused the nuns to cherish the memory of their kind and humble foundress.

Her husband, Count Burchard, also lived in the nuns' grateful memory; they always had a mass offered for him on the anniversary of his death. Once during this mass, St. Mechtild saw him wearing a robe on which appeared the images of all the former members of the congregation and also of those who would later join it. His crown had a corresponding number of gold fleurons. On another anniversary she saw him richly clothed and adorned with jewels signifying a great variety of virtues. When she asked him in amazement how he had acquired such graces, he replied: "Not by my own works but by the goodness of God and the merits of the congregation that I loved so dearly." He explained to Mechtild that it was on the entry into heaven of her sister, "the magnificent and royal Abbess Gertrude," that he had been so attired.

This Abbess Gertrude was the second superior of the community. Her predecessor, Cunegunde of Halberstadt, "devout and God-fearing," had come with seven companions to Mansfeld, the home of their founders, Count Burchard and his wife, Elizabeth. During these times of baronial wars, however, proximity to a castle was a danger rather than a protection; therefore, at the suggestion of the foundress, the community made their first move, to nearby Rodardsdorf. Elizabeth, who had become a widow shortly after the establishment of the community, also went to Rodardsdorf where she died in 1240.

In 1251, Cunegunde was succeeded by Gertrude von Hackeborn, who though only nineteen had been unanimously elected. Seven years later, in 1258, a shortage of water necessitated the community's second removal. The site of the new establishment was Helfta, near Eisleben, on land given by the brothers of the abbess. The ground was fertile and gently sloping. Woods, fields, and orchard were threaded by spring-fed streams flowing into the lake of Seeburg.

A distinguished company of ecclesiastics and nobles assisted at the solemn entry of the community into its new home. The guests included the two counts of Mansfeld and Querfurt, sons-in-law of Burchard; Rupert, the Archbishop of Magdeburg; and Vulrad, Archbishop of Halberstadt. The last-named celebrated the mass and presided at the reception of several young women into the community. Among those received were Sophia and Elizabeth, granddaughters of the founders, both of whom figure in the later history of the monastery.

Despite the patronage of noble families, life was far from easy at Helfta. The rigors of the daily routine seem scarcely worth mentioning in view of the far greater ordeals which the community suffered: the pressure of debts, losses by theft, and exposure to assault.

During and after the Great Interregnum poverty and the terror of the robber-barons demoralized Saxony and Thuringia. Many of the nuns were related to the barons, but such family ties afforded no protection; on the contrary, they subjected the community to involvement in local feuds. One of these disputes resulted in an outrageous attack against Helfta in 1284 by Gebhardt von Mansfeld whose sister and cousins were members of the community. With a band of followers he invaded the cloister, ate meat there on Good Friday, and behaved with such violence that he was excommunicated by Pope Martin IV. The reason for this assault is not known—"a family quarrel," says one commentator. Gebhardt died suddenly the next year, and at the request of his widow, Irmingarde von Schwartzburg, he was eventually buried within the monastery in the mortuary chapel built by his father. His long-suffering sister Sophia was elected abbess in 1291. Three years later, his son, who had bequeathed the monastery twenty-nine acres of wooded ground, was accompanied to his grave by all the nuns in solemn procession. A more arresting example of the peculiar family involvements of some medieval religious communities would be hard to find.

Throughout such vicissitudes the Abbess Gertrude not only governed her large community with calm fortitude, but as Stierli declares, brought it to "the highest level of feminine culture known to the Middle Ages."[1] It is understandable, therefore, that her death in 1291 was a calamity. The account of her last hours is filled with expressions of sorrow and affection. With loving minuteness it is recorded that she had governed her monastery "for 40 years and 11 days" when she was seized by her last illness.

The successor of the Abbess Gertrude was Sophia von Mansfeld. During her incumbency the war between Adolph of Nassau and his rivals devastated Thuringia. A detail in the life of St. Mechtild shows how the members of the community were involved in the disorders of the time.

Once a lady who feared for her husband, knowing that his enemies were planning to ambush him on his journey and keep him in captivity until their prisoners were released, begged the saint to pray for him. Mechtild prayed, and received a consoling answer which reassured the lady. On another occasion when a similar danger threatened her husband, the same lady was consoled by St. Mechtild's prophetic words: "He will go through much more adver-

[1] Josef Stierli, "Devotion to the Sacred Heart from the End of Patristic Times to St. Margaret Mary" in *Heart of the Saviour* (New York, 1958) p. 72.

5

sity and peril, but our Lord will preserve him from captivity and serious injury."

A grievous trial for the sisters was the interdict imposed by the canons of Halberstadt about 1296, the fifth year of Sophia's term as abbess. The exact reason is not known. St. Mechtild says that while the see of Halberstadt was vacant, the canons placed an interdict upon the community, "greatly afflicting it on account of certain pecuniary matters." This statement would imply that the financial problems of the convent became more numerous. The closing of their church, the silencing of organ and chant, the deprivation of the sacraments and of mass, profoundly saddened all the sisters.

In 1298, because of poor health, the Abbess Sophia resigned her office and an interregnum of five years followed, after which Jutta of Halberstadt was elected.

During this interregnum, the community lost its most outstanding member, St. Gertrude the Great, who died in 1301 at the age of forty-five. The golden age of the community had passed, but not its trials.

In 1342, Albert of Brunswig invaded Helfta with a large army. He had been elected to the episcopacy of Halberstadt, but the Holy See did not confirm his election. Instead, the Sovereign Pontiff suggested as suitable alternates, first Giselbert of Holzsac and then Albert of Mansfeld. When the latter was confirmed by the Holy See as bishop of Halberstadt, his sister Luitgard was abbess at Helfta. The would-be bishop, Albert of Brunswig, stormed the convent and with his own hand set fire to it, while his men broke into the cloister to destroy vestments, books, ornaments, and everything else they could find. Some German verses are extant, lamenting the destruction of the monastery and the calamity of the disputed election.

Four years later, in 1346, Burchard IV of Mansfeld, father of the Abbess Luitgard, transferred the community to Eisleben, its fourth and last site. The exodus occurred on the feast of St. Severin, which fell on the Sunday when the Mass *Da Pacem* is sung. Leaving their damaged monastery, the community must have chanted the words with profound feeling.

Little is known of the nuns of Helfta from their transfer to Eisleben in 1346 until 1451 when Sophia of Stolburg, the abbess, compiled some notes on the history of her congregation. In them she mentioned that she drew her information "from our chronicle and from our own certain knowledge." Unfortunately the cloister record is lost, and, according to Grössler, the notes cannot be accepted as wholly reliable.[2]

Approximately fifty years later, about 1500, a reform of the rule was introduced under the auspices of the Abbess Catherine von Watzdorff. It was this Catherine whom Luther castigated in a pamphlet, calling her "a second Jezebel." His pamphlet, published in 1524, tells of the "miraculous escape" of a young nun, Florentina, who fled from the convent to Wittenberg to join the Lutherans. The fury of the peasants against the monastery at the time of the uprising in 1525 is thought to have been inspired by this work. During the Peasants' Rebellion, the Abbess Catherine was forced to escape to "old" Helfta. In retaliation perhaps, the books and manuscripts of the community were thrown into beer vats.

According to the Solesmes editors of the writings of St. Gertrude and St. Mechtild *(Revelationes Gertrudianae ac Mechtildianae)* it is not known whether the Abbess Cath-

---

[2] H. Grössler, *Die Blütezeit des Klosters Helfta bei Eisleben* (Eisleben, 1887) p. 7.

erine had a successor; however Grössler names two: Anna von Watzdorff and Walberg Reuber.[3]

With the intrusion of an heretical prelate in 1546, the religious family of St. Gertrude and St. Mechtild became extinct.

More than 300 years later, the next mention of the community is made on November 17, 1868, the feastday of St. Gertrude, when the buildings of "new" Helfta were purchased for the foundation of the Benedictine monastery of Trud Kloster, named after the great saint of Helfta. Mother St. Michael (Elizabeth Falger), the prioress, together with a group of nuns from the convent of Osnabruck, took possession of the property and were cordially welcomed by the entire city whose Catholic residents assisted in the restoration of the monastery.

Severe hardship awaited the sisters however, and very soon after, the prioress, Mother St. Michael, was stricken by paralysis. She died on July 13, 1873. A year later the May Laws of 1874 deprived the community of their property and it was not until 1890 that the site could be repurchased for the construction of a church dedicated to St. Gertrude.

According to Father Walter, the acting curate of the parish of Eisleben-Helfta, relics of St. Gertrude may be buried under the foundation of the church named for her in the Klosterplatz of Eisleben. Dean Westerman, the builder, had a large structure razed, but found no trace of the saint's body. To this day, no one knows whether the nuns who left Helfta brought the relics with them.

As recently as 1916, some of the buildings at "old" Helfta were still standing. What had once been the convent church, however, had been transformed into a gran-

[3] Ibid. p. 35.

ary by the Lutherans who lowered the roof, removed the vaulting, and blocked up many of the lancet windows.

As has been mentioned previously, the ruins of the old convent church are now protected as an historical monument. Sunday Mass is offered at Helfta in an evangelical church for approximately 350 Catholics who live in the area.

LIFE AT HELFTA

Helfta's "Golden Age" began with the election of the Abbess Gertrude von Hackeborn in 1251. The character of the abbess, exceptional in youth, became even more admirable during her long term of office. It is some evidence of the reputation of Helfta during her regime that the Teutonic Knights at Halle obtained from her a statement of "confraternity" entitling them to a share in the merits of the prayers, vigils, and other good works of the community. Indeed, religious observance held first place in the life of this learned and cultured community.

Regarding the spiritual origins of the community at Helfta, a minor debate has arisen as to whether the nuns lived under the Cistercian or the Benedictine rule. Mme. Ancelet-Hustache, in her study of the documents relating to Helfta, finds that the evidence for the Cistercian claim is too strong to be disputed.[4]

The latest editor of Gertrude's *Exercises,* however, explains that although the original foundation was made by Cistercian nuns, the community itself did not belong to the order since the General Chapter of 1228 forbade the founding and direction of communities of nuns. "It follows," therefore, the editor concludes, "that Helfta must

[4] Jeanne Ancelet-Hustache, *Mechtilde de Magdeburg* (Paris, 1926) p. 59.

have been one of the many autonomous abbeys of Benedictine nuns that flourished in Germany in the thirteenth century." Reconciling these two assertions, Dom
Doyère's opinion is that in St. Gertrude's day "the discipline and spirituality of Helfta were undoubtedly of Cistercian inspiration, while at the same time, thanks to its
independence, the monastery observed certain customs
of its own."[5]

Cistercians or Benedictines as they might be, the sisters
at Helfta were undoubtedly influenced by the Dominicans.
The proximity of the Dominican convents of Halle and
Magdeburg makes it more than likely that they were the
usual preachers at Helfta. Likewise, under papal order
and later, in 1256, by ruling of the Chapter of Florence,
the Dominican friars were required to act as the spiritual
directors not only of Dominican nuns but of the members
of the other orders as well. Greatly outnumbered by their
charges and impeded in their studies by this obligation, the
Dominicans made many efforts to be relieved of this duty.
They were briefly successful in 1252 when Innocent III
granted their request, but two years later he withdrew his
permission. As mentioned previously the Chapter of Florence also confirmed this obligation. Moreover, Herman
von Minden, Provincial of the Dominicans from 1286 to
1290 recommended that learned friars be chosen as the
directors of well-educated nuns. According to Mme. Ancelet-Hustache, "The Friars Preachers knew how to direct
these intelligent women and to develop their inclination to
contemplation."[6] Indeed, Denifle sees an important con-
nection between the rise of German mysticism and the

[5] *The Exercises of St. Gertrude,* ed. A Benedictine Nun of Regina
Laudis (Westminster, Maryland, 1956) xv.
[6] Ancelet-Hustache, p. 22.

papal order enjoining the Friars Preachers to assume the spiritual direction of women.

The sermons which the sisters heard at Helfta must have been basically Thomistic in content since the General Chapter of 1278 imposed the teaching of St. Thomas on all Dominicans. It is interesting to note in this context that it was probably a Dominican who preached the sermon that inspired Gertrude to ask for the wound of divine love. (This incident will be recounted in a later chapter.)

There is little evidence of any notable lack of fervor among nuns at Helfta. However, in her writings, St. Mechtild does speak of slothfulness in assisting at divine service. St. Gertrude herself once fell asleep at Mass and was awakened by the bell at the consecration. The association of the nuns with noble families—relatives of the sisters and of the pupils—may also have led to some excessive interest in "worldly affairs." Indeed, both St. Gertrude and St. Mechtild show minute knowledge of social ceremonies in their writings. Although the usual mediocrities probably impaired the dedication of the community, the general impression of Helfta is that of an admirable conventual household.

In the busy life of the monastery, even the hours spent in the chapel were seldom undisturbed. (St. Mechtild was filled with compassion for the overburdened portress who was frequently summoned from mass to attend to guests.) Care of the sick, moreover, was accepted as a necessary duty in religious houses and the charity with which it was given was an index to the fervor of the community. St. Gertrude herself is said to have overtaxed her strength in her devotion to the sick. In her writings, she refers several times to the skill of doctors in restoring health through potions. Bloodletting was a regular practice and usually took place in the spring.

In a community which numbered more than 100 members, the amount of manual work was considerable. All the sisters undertook such tasks as spinning and the ordinary duties of a household. The abbess was often the first at work. Many passages in the writings of the Saints Gertrude and Mechtild testify to the industry of the hard-working community. Realistic scenes of homely household activity emerge from Gertrude's references to steam from a cooking vessel, the difficulty of handling flour without getting it on oneself, the use of iron hammers to remove rust, and the practice of inserting a prop into a bundle of faggots. Even mishaps are cited: when one is dyeing a cloth with saffron, anything else falling into the dye is likewise colored; a pot used in cooking may catch fire. The appetizing odor of food, the rapidity with which fresh bread soaks up mead, the uselessness of a wooden knife—all of these domestic images figure in Gertrude's forceful comparisons.

The importance of music in the monastic life at Helfta is also evident. In the Rule of St. Benedict many chapters deal with the proper performance of the Divine Office. In addition to this religious exercise, it was the custom at Helfta, as at Cluny, to recite additional psalms which greatly prolonged the Office. These *Psalmi familiares* were said in choir at the beginning or at the end of each canonical hour. Evidently at Helfta certain of these special psalms were assigned to one nun who said them outside the hours of office, either by herself or with several others. The offices of the Trinity, of the Blessed Virgin, and of the saints were recited as private devotions. Among the hymns mentioned in Gertrude's writings are *Jesu Nostra Redemptio, Rex Christe Factor Omnium, O Crux Ave* (from the hymn of Terce), *Gloria Laus, Veni Creator, Quem Terra*

Pontus Aethera, and several stanzas of *Jesu Dulcis Memoria.* (When she speaks of the *Ave Stella Maris,* she is probably referring to the hymn now known as the *Ave Maris Stella.*) It was the custom, at this time, to "farce" certain psalms by adding prayers after each verse. This was done with the *Benedicite* when the community was in fear of an armed attack. For the souls of the dead, the sisters recited the Great Psalter, which is also a "farced" arrangement of the psalms with long prayers after each one. Gertrude once asked Christ why this Psalter was so advantageous to the souls of the departed and so pleasing to him, for it seemed to her that the exceedingly long prayers caused more weariness than devotion. He replied that his intense desire for the deliverance of those souls caused him to release great numbers of them from Purgatory when the Psalter was recited.

Although common prayers and the necessary menial activities of the monastery occupied several hours of each day, the community at Helfta also spent much time in study and teaching.

Since the time of St. Boniface and his disciple St. Lioba more than five centuries earlier, a strong tradition of education for women had developed in Germany. (Of St. Lioba it is recorded that during her noonday rest she used to correct the mispronunciations of the novices who read the Latin scriptures to her.) Franz Anton Specht in his history of learning in Germany before the middle of the thirteenth century declares that many women were devoted to serious study. Cloistered nuns in particular, bound by rule to choral prayer and spiritual reading, had to be skilled in chant and have some knowledge of Latin. That the cloister also helped to raise the level of intellectual life in the world is apparent since many girls who did not intend to become nuns were educated in the convent schools.[7]

As for the studies pursued by the nuns and their students, they were, according to Specht, as rigorous as those of clerics. Ordinarily the novices were instructed in the courses of the trivium: grammar, rhetoric, and logic. It was not unusual for them, however, to advance to the quadrivium: arithmetic, geometry, astronomy, and music. Theology was also included in the curriculum. In addition, citations in monastic literature show that the writers were familiar with the authors of classical antiquity. Copying manuscripts also required the ability to correct mistakes.

According to G. H. Putnam, "It is difficult to estimate the extent of the services rendered by feminine hands to learning and to history throughout the Middle Ages. They brought to the work a dexterity, an elegance of attainment, and an assiduity which the monks themselves could not attain, and some of the most beautiful specimens of calligraphy which have been preserved from the Middle Ages are the work of nuns."[8]

It is relevant to note that Abbo of Fleury associates the work of the copyist with prayer and fasting as a means of mortification.

Original composition as well as manuscript copying occupied some of the nuns at Helfta. The monastic letter was a recognized literary genre during the Middle Ages. In addition to their spiritual treatises, St. Gertrude and the two Mechtilds also wrote such letters. In fact, some of St. Mechtild's correspondence is quoted in *The Book of Special Grace.*

[7] *Geschichte des Unterrichtswesen in Deutschland bis zur Mitte des XIII Jahrhunderts* (Stuttgart, 1885) pp. 256-257.
[8] G. H. Putnam, *Books and Their Makers During the Middle Ages* (New York, 1896) I, pp. 52-53.

St. Gertrude was perhaps the most scholarly member of the community at Helfta, but the nun who wrote the saint's biography (Book One of the *Legatus*) quotes Bede, Augustine, Bernard, Gregory, Benedict, and Hugh of St. Victor.

It should not be forgotten, moreover, that this steady pursuit of learning and holiness was carried on despite the distractions inseparable from conducting a school, the pressure of acute financial anxieties, and periods of grave danger when marauding nobles threatened the convent. It is largely owing to the calm stability of the nuns under the leadership of their second abbess, Gertrude von Hackeborn, that Helfta reached and maintained its intellectual and spiritual eminence.

The Women of Helfta

THE BELOVED ABBESS:
GERTRUDE VON HACKEBORN

Gertrude von Hackeborn, abbess and countess, ruled the community at Helfta for forty years. During that time she was able to impress her own spiritual and intellectual ideals on a community which eventually numbered more than one hundred members.

The character and personality of the abbess inspired so much confidence that many of the distinguished families of the region sent their daughters to her to be educated. Important names—Mansfeld, Querfurt and Stolberg—appear in surviving documents.

The abbess herself and her sister Mechtild belonged to a prominent family, the barons of Hackeborn and lords of Wippra. The site of the family estate near Halberstadt is still known by its ancient name although the line became extinct in the fifteenth century.

In addition to the abbess and her sister, other members of the family—perhaps cousins or nieces—joined the community at Helfta, for in a panegyric of the Abbess Gertrude it is said that her affection and kindness to all the sisters was so great that an observer could not have discovered which ones were related to her. She showed the same affection towards the children in the monastery school, and they loved her dearly. It was said of her that she was "gentle with the little ones, holy and discreet with the young, wise and cheerful with the old."

At the same time, the Abbess Gertrude maintained a high level of intellectual achievement among her charges. Free from any morbid mistrust of learning, she was known to say that if the study of letters should be neglected, soon the Scriptures would no longer be understood, and monastic life would begin to decay. She spared no effort to obtain books, and insisted that all her nuns, especially the younger and less instructed ones, be diligent in their studies. With St. Bernard she believed that "the spouse of the Lord should not be a dolt." It may well be that at Helfta all in the community were intended to become "literatae"—the term used to designate those capable of taking part in the office.

The abbess was also a prudent manager, utilizing to the full the resources of Helfta. During her long term of office there were many benefactions recorded.

Her solicitude extended to a second convent that she founded at Hedersleben where in 1253, only two years after her election, she sent twelve nuns from Rodardsdorf. A donation of land from her brothers had made this enterprise possible.

A document exists which declares that the provost Otto, the Abbess Gertrude, and the chapter of the community pledge themselves willingly to readmit "our twelve beloved sisters" if at any time the pressure of poverty or the destruction of the property at Hedersleben should make such a return desirable. The troubled times in which the document was drawn up—it is dated 1262, nine years after the new foundation—make such a precaution understandable.

17

It has been noted that because of the similarity of names, this venerable abbess has sometimes been incorrectly identified with St. Gertrude the Great, and this error has been perpetuated in the office of the saint. In the Second Nocturn it is asserted that St. Gertrude was born at Eisleben and entered the convent at Rodardsdorf. This confusion of the saint with her abbess recalls the sardonic French expression: "to lie like a Second Nocturn." The error has caused many writers to refer to St. Gertrude as a countess and artists to depict her with the abbatial crozier.

As an example of the charity of the abbess, it is recorded that in her last illness she insisted on being carried to the bedside of another nun who was also ill, and though so weak herself that she was unable to speak, showed her affection and sympathy by gestures.

During this illness, since the abbess had always been as active as her increasing corpulency would permit, it pained her greatly that she could no longer work with her hands. In her distress, she appealed to St. Gertrude, who told her: "The King of goodness does not require that his chosen one work on her adornment when he pleases to take her hands into his own. What he desires above all is that she be always ready to accomplish his will. His divine Heart looks at her with pleasure whether she is patiently enduring her illness which keeps her from working, or occupying herself with her duty whenever suffering gives her some respite."

When the Abbess Gertrude found that her illness impeded her in the discharge of her office, she wished to surrender it, but she was told that God had left her the partial use of her faculties in order that she might still govern her daughters, even to the extent of correcting those who did wrong. It saddened her to see the sisters tiring themselves in her care when there was no hope of her recovery.

Christ, however, said to St. Gertrude: "Let her rejoice that I make use of her to increase their merits, for I regard as done for myself all the services that she receives and all the love that is shown her even by a single word."

The abbess Gertrude von Hackeborn died in 1291 after a five-month illness—"minor apoplexy"—according to the contemporary account.

After her death, she appeared in glory to St. Gertrude, holding a lily and other flowers in one hand, while with the other she led the spirits of all the members of the community who had preceded her in death. St. Gertrude learned that Christ felt compassion for the bereaved nuns, and she saw the abbess offering their tears in a golden chalice. This favor was granted as a reward for the vigilance and discretion she had shown in governing. In fact, the grief of these sisters was largely motivated by the fear that after the death of so excellent a superior, religious observance would be less perfect.

In the *Book of Special Grace,* it is said that Gertrude was one of the two abbesses (Cunegunde was the other) who received a heavenly reward because none of those in their charge had been lost.

Such was the woman whose influence not only made Helfta a center of culture and holiness in thirteenth-century Saxony, but also created for her monastic family a true home.

Of more enduring fame than their abbess, however, are the three mystics of Helfta—St. Gertrude the Great whose biography will be treated in detail in Book Two, St. Mechtild von Hackeborn, and Mechtild von Magdeburg.

THE FIERY BEGUINE:
MECHTILD VON MAGDEBURG

Unlike St. Mechtild von Hackeborn and St. Gertrude

19

the Great, Mechtild von Magdeburg, third of the mystics of Helfta, is not ranked among the saints. Nevertheless, through her writings, she too has brought fame to the convent which became her final home.

Born about 1210 in the Archbishopric of Magdeburg, Mechtild was, as she says, the best-loved of her family, members of the ruling class. When she was twelve, she received "a greeting from the Holy Spirit," and from that time on, she tells us, longed to be regarded with contempt. Her wish was to be granted in full measure.

At twenty-three, Mechtild left her family in order to give herself to God without distraction. For many years, thereafter, she lived as a beguine[1] in the city of Magdeburg.

Although Mechtild was not without friends and admirers, her writings provoked such opposition that she was forced to leave Magdeburg for Helfta about 1285. The following episode recounted by one of the nuns in her memoir of St. Gertrude is considered to refer to Mechtild von Magdeburg.

Having gone to the convent, the account relates, Mechtild prayed that God might direct her to someone there who could assist her spiritually. She was given to understand that a person who would come and take a place near her was a true and faithful spouse of Christ, preferred by him before all the others. Gertrude came, seated herself near Mechtild, and spoke to her, but the saint's manner was so humble that the visitor could not believe her to be the one designated by Christ. Returning to her prayer with many complaints, she was informed that Gertrude was in-

---

[1] The word "beguine" is derived from the name of Lambert le Bègue, a priest of Liège, who counseled women to live in communities and minister to the sick and the poor. These women were not cloistered nor were they obliged to bring a dowry. In the 13th century, beguines were numerous—there were thousands of them in Germany alone, where the Dominicans took a special interest in them.

deed the true and faithful spouse whom he preferred. Subsequently, the beguine had a conversation with St. Mechtild, sister of the abbess, and was enchanted by her. Why, she wondered, had God exalted Gertrude above this admirable and holy nun? He answered: "I am working great things in Mechtild, but those which I am working and shall work in Gertrude are far greater."[2]

Shortly after this visit to Helfta, the beguine, although advanced in age, entered the convent. Her brother Baldwin, sub-prior at the Dominican convent in Halle, may have urged her to take this step. (The Dominicans at Halle were evidently well known to the community at Helfta.) Once there, the old beguine was received by the nuns with a truly aristocratic acceptance of eccentricity. That they respected, loved, and ministered to her is evidence of their charity and her holiness.

Soon after her arrival, Mechtild underwent a serious illness which resulted in blindness. The nuns nursed her compassionately, but she was in anguish at the thought of her uselessness. "Lord! What can I do in this convent?" she cried. "Thou shalt enlighten and teach and shalt stay here in great honor," was the answer.

Despite this sense of uselessness and especially after the storms she had endured at Magdeburg, Mechtild found healing and refreshment in the atmosphere of Helfta. Her gratitude broke forth in a series of exclamations:

> Lord, I thank thee that since in thy love thou hast taken from me all earthly riches, thou now clothest and feedest me through the goodness of others. . . . Lord, I thank thee that since thou hast taken from me the sight of my eyes,

[2] If the visit occurred shortly before the entrance of Mechtild von Magdeburg into the community, it would have been when St. Gertrude was 28 or 29.

thou servest me through the eyes of others. Lord, I thank thee that since thou hast taken from me the power of my hands . . . and the power of my heart, thou now servest me with the hands and hearts of others.

Lord, I pray thee for them. Reward them here on earth with thy divine love that they may faithfully serve and please thee with all virtue till they come to a happy end.[3]

Long before her arrival at Helfta the old beguine had witnessed civil disorder. "I was commanded to pray very earnestly for the need there now is in Saxony and Thuringia," she says. (Lucy Menzies, the English translator of *The Flowing Light of the Godhead,* surmises that this sentence was written in 1270 when the dissolution of the Rhineland provinces caused general agitation.)

Yet there was trouble at Helfta, and Mechtild shared in the trials of the community. "My heart is full of pity for the troubles of this community in which I am," she writes. Evidently one of the ordeals was the dissemination of slanderous reports about the sisters. Christ reminded Mechtild that he was likewise slandered despite his innocence; therefore false accusations should not grieve them.

It is good to know that despite the unsettled times, the fiery yet humble Mechtild found friends to console her in her old age and blindness. Both St. Gertrude and St. Mechtild speak of her with respect, and the dying words of the poor refugee from Magdeburg testify to her appreciation of her new religious family: "I take leave of all my dear friends. I thank God and them that they have been my help in need. Were I to be longer here, I should ever be ashamed of the lack of virtue they must have seen in me." Death came to Mechtild in 1297, in her eighty-eighth year.

It is recorded in *The Book of Special Grace* by St. Mech-

[3] *The Revelations of Mechtild of Magdeburg* trans. Lucy Menzies (London, 1953) pp. 261-262. All quotations from the writings of Mechtild von Magdeburg are taken from this translation.

tild von Hackeborn, sister of the abbess, that she saw in a vision a heavenly festival with virgins dancing around the Savior. They sang "new songs" in which the congregation at Helfta was praised. "Sister M." appeared with these virgins, illuminated by a ray of light from the Sacred Heart to signify the gift of divine love. Editors conjecture that this "Sister M." was Mechtild von Magdeburg.

THE FLOWING LIGHT OF THE GODHEAD

After many years of austerity and a severe illness as well, Mechtild von Magdeburg felt compelled to write an account of her experiences. She declares: "I cannot write nor do I wish to write. Of the heavenly things God has shown me, I can speak but a little word, not more than a honey bee can carry away on its foot from an overflowing jar . . . I am not expert in writing, but now I fear before God if I keep silent about these things, and before ignorant people if I speak."

These "things" were, in particular, the secret ways of God with her soul, and the ill-conduct of her contemporaries, specifically the clergy and religious of Magdeburg.

In discussing the secret ways of God with her soul, Mechtild used the language of court and chivalry, sometimes breaking into lyrical rhythms of great beauty. For example,

> I cannot dance, O Lord, unless thou lead me.
> If thou wilt that I leap joyfully
> Thou must thyself first dance and sing!
> — Then will I leap for love
> From love to knowledge
> From knowledge to fruition
> From fruition to beyond all human sense
> There will I remain
> And circle evermore.

Several other passages of this work are reminiscent of

Dante—for example: "Up on the heights there soared a maiden who was like a golden eagle. She was surrounded by a heavenly host, and she shone and taught and trained all these maidens to serve their lady the Queen." (The Queen here symbolizes the human person; the maidens are the virtues; the eagle-maiden, love.)

The wisdom as well as the ecstasy of love is expressed in Mechtild's writings. She says: "The nature of love is such that it overflows at first in sweetness, then it becomes rich in understanding, thirdly, it abounds in desolation." This teaching becomes specific in her description of the spiritual garments of the bride of Christ: her daily apparel is made of fasts, vigils, disciplines, confessions, tears, and prayers; her wedding garments are temptations, maladies, and all other sufferings that prepare her for the bridegroom.

Mechtild's second theme, the reproach of her contemporaries, aroused much hostility against her. "Ah, foolish beguines!" she exclaims. "How can ye be so bold that ye do not tremble before our Almighty Judge when, as so often, ye receive the Body of the Lord as a matter of blind habit!" It grieved her to the heart "that spiritual people are so imperfect. When God wishes to set their hearts on fire with love so that others may know and love God in them, these favored ones refuse and say 'Nay! I can be of more use in outward things'."

Some of her admonitions to superiors show shrewd practicality joined to zeal for God's honor:

> Thou shalt also go to the kitchen
> To make sure that the needful provision is good . . .
> No hungry priest may sing sweetly
> Nor study deeply—
> Thus might our Lord lack the service
> Which is his due.

Mechtild was well aware of the antagonism she inspired. She says "I was warned about the book and told by many that it should not be preserved but rather thrown to the flames." Notwithstanding these threats Mechtild continued her writing over a period of fifteen years.

While still a beguine at Magdeburg, Mechtild had completed the first six books of *Das Fliessende Licht der Gottheit (The Flowing Light of the Godhead)*. Later, during her stay at Helfta, she dictated the seventh book to the nuns there. Unfortunately, the original manuscript, written in Low German, does not survive. Pages of the work were collected by Mechtild's friend, Heinrich von Halle, lector of Neu-Ruppin, who had been a pupil of St. Albert the Great. (Heinrich was greatly impressed by her "masculine style.") The lector arranged the loose sheets according to his own ideas, however, and so it is not certain that the present sequence is chronological. He also made a Latin version, now at Basel, but it lacks the vigor of the original Low German.

In the fourteenth century, a secular priest, Heinrich von Nordlingen, made a High German translation of Mechtild's work.

As has already been mentioned, the writings of Mechtild von Magdeburg were widely criticized during her lifetime, but she who had longed for contempt was concerned only for God's honor. In her desolation, after her works were attacked, Mechtild prayed: "Ah, Lord! seeing thou hast taken from me all that I had of thee, give me of thy grace the gift every dog has by nature, that of being true to my master in my need when deprived of all consolation."

In Mechtild's last illness, St. Gertrude, who was at her deathbed, was distressed to see that the old nun's mind was wandering and that some members of the community were skeptical of her revelations. For this reason, she prayed that after the death of Mechtild von Magdeburg miracles might occur to silence her critics. In answer, Christ made clear to Gertrude that his triumphs could be achieved without signs and portents.

THE CONVENTUAL HOUSEHOLD

Other gifted nuns, members of the community at Helfta, were three descendants of the founder: "Sophia Senior" (so called to distinguish her from her cousin of the same name) who transcribed many books; her sister Elizabeth, a talented painter and illuminator (it may have been she who painted the crucifix from which a ray of light issued when St. Gertrude received the wound of divine love); and their cousin Sophia, who was later abbess.

Associated with these sisters were others whose names have not come down to us: the nun who recorded St. Gertrude's *Legatus* from dictation or from her notes; the one who assisted in compiling the account of St. Mechtild von Hackeborn, *The Book of Special Grace;* and various members of the community whose chance words and actions, or whose deaths are recorded in the books written at Helfta.

Intimate glimpses of the types of personality found in the community at Helfta are given in accounts of the human frailties of the sisters whose deaths Gertrude noted in her writings. One of them had taken too much pleasure in material things—specifically, a bedspread embroidered with gold. (The nineteenth-century English translator is convinced that the nun could not have owned such an article, and that her fault must have occurred before she entered the convent. It seems more probable that after she was a nun she might have taken satisfaction in the thought of her former possessions and have spoken of them complacently to her companions.)

A second instance of the slight imperfections of these holy women is given in the *Legatus*. St. Gertrude relates that only twelve days after the demise of the beloved Abbess Gertrude, she was followed in death by another sister who had endeared herself to all by her innocence, fervor, and friendliness. Those who had lived with her mourned her passing and the suddenness of their loss made it harder to bear. The sister had prayed that she might enter heaven without delay. But as she was young, "and in time of youth one is seldom free from slight negligences," she was purified from these faults by experiencing a great fear of the devil in her last illness. Her patience in sickness and this ordeal of fear made her ready to see God.

Among the deaths recorded by St. Gertrude are those of two sisters, members of a noble family, who died within twenty days of each other. The younger sister, St. Gertrude comments, received a particular reward in heaven because of her devotion to the Blessed Sacrament. (This means that there were at least three pairs of sisters in the convent at this time: the Abbess Gertrude and St. Mechtild; Sophia and Elizabeth, descendants of the founder; and these two, who are designated merely as M. and E.)

St. Gertrude also mentions another nun of Helfta who although notable for her patience and fervor, had been unwilling to go to confession, even though seriously ill, because she had no grave sins. When the priest came, she pretended to be asleep, so as not to have to speak with him. Before her death, she atoned for this fault when, having asked for the priest, she was unable to make her confession. St. Gertrude mentions that after her death Christ received her soul with great tenderness, in this way consoling her for the disquiet she had experienced on seeing

27

another sister who was ill being given more care than she herself had received. (The community had mistakenly supposed that the latter was not in immediate danger.) After her death, which occurred a month before that of her companion, this nun was asked by Christ what she wished him to do for the other sister. Her generous answer was "Give her all that you have given me, for I can think of nothing better."

Of the sister who died later, St. Gertrude notes that she was admirable for her innocence and her exact observance of the rule; she had, however, during her illness taken undue pleasure in unnecessary articles, little gifts from the other nuns, and their consoling remarks. In regard to both these sisters, the saint learned that even though one had served God longer than the other, the younger sister might have surpassed her in merit by greater fervor, a more upright intention, or by surmounting greater obstacles.

A curious little sidelight in the relations of Gertrude with this younger nun is provided by the account of a conversation between them. Seeing the spirit of her departed companion looking at her affectionately the saint said: "You always loved me. Why is it then, that you seemed not to take my advice when you were in your last illness?" Acknowledging the truth of St. Gertrude's words, the dead sister added, "Now your prayers for me have more efficacy since you have offered them purely from charity and the love of God."

The exceptional sanctity of some of the saint's companions may be exemplified by the holy death of another sister. She had already entered into her last agony when she bade a loving farewell to her community and promised to pray for everyone. Then turning to God, she said: "O Savior, you know all my secrets; you know how much I wished to spend my strength in serving you faithfully until old age and decrepitude. But since I see that you wish me to go to you, all my desire is changed into the thirst of seeing you; and this ardent longing sweetens the bitterness of death. Yet if it were your pleasure, I should gladly endure my sufferings until the day of doom, even if we were now at the beginning of the world. I know that you wish to call me to my repose today, but I entreat your kindness to wait until my pains have made satisfaction for those souls in purgatory whose deliverance you most desire. You know, O my Savior, that I make nothing of my own merits, but consider in this only your glory." When the infirmarian wished to straighten out the contracted knees of the dying nun, she was told, "I shall offer this sacrifice myself to my crucified Savior." After a moment, she asked to have the Passion read to her and pointed out the place where the reader should begin: "Then Jesus, lifting up his eyes to heaven. . . ." (John, XVII, 1) "for" she said, "if you begin with 'Before the festal day,' (John XIII, 1) there will not be time to finish." At the words, "And bowing down his head, he gave up his spirit," she asked for the crucifix, and having kissed the wounds of Christ, she died peacefully.

Gertrude's comments on the deaths of some lay brothers bring to our attention the various male workers of the community. These members of the conventual household included a provost, some brothers *(fratres conversi)* under the jurisdiction of the abbess, and a number of farm laborers.

In recording the deaths of the lay brothers Gertrude mentions the following details of interest. When one of these brothers was in his agony, St. Gertrude had been much occupied; after his death she reproached herself for her neglect, for he had been more faithful and devoted to the monastery than had any other brother. His kindness had been shown in many ways, such as giving alms to the poor, little gifts to children, and fruit to the sick.

A certain brother Herman had also served the community faithfully, but had been too much attached to his own will, so that when he did anyone a favor it was, so to say, on his own terms. He had also been somewhat slow to forgive those who had injured him, and for a long time after the offense, he would meet them with a severe expression. Nevertheless, he had won such affection by his faithful service to the community that the nuns prayed fervently for his recovery and shed tears at his death.

Another brother, designated simply as "F" was obliged to expiate in the next world his fault of having worked to obtain various articles without the superior's permission, and then having concealed them. St. Gertrude learned that all those persons who had worked for the monastery received after death a great reward for their services, far more, in fact, than came to them for an even longer service in other places.

*   *   *

These were the women—and men—of Helfta, companions, advisors, and friends to two of the greatest mystics of the Church—St. Gertrude the Great and St. Mechtild von Hackeborn.

The Nightingale of Christ

When Mechtild von Hackeborn was born in 1241 or 1242, she was so frail that it was feared she might die unbaptized, and her nurses carried her posthaste to a priest who was about to say mass. After baptizing the infant, he said: "Why are you afraid? This child will certainly not die, but she will become a saintly religious in whom God will work many wonders and she will end her days in a good old age."

Mechtild's entry into religious life was as precipitate as her baptism. The family home was near Rodardsdorf where the community which she was destined to enter was then situated. One day, when Mechtild was seven, her mother brought her to visit her elder sister Gertrude, the future abbess of the community. With the compelling charm that she was never to lose, the little girl went to each sister in turn, begging to stay. When the nuns joined their pleas to hers, the mother finally yielded—how unwillingly one can well imagine—and went home without her. As many of the children in the convent school were her own age or younger, Mechtild did not lack for playmates in her new surroundings.

In 1258, when she was about seventeen, the sisters moved from Rodardsdorf to Helfta. Although she was already a member of the community at that time, it is possible that Mechtild's formal consecration did not occur until 1266, for this ceremony was not performed until the candidate was twenty-five. Since St. Gertrude had been brought to Helfta some years before, she would have been about ten years old then, and was undoubtedly a spectator at this impressive rite.

Eventually, Mechtild taught the children in the abbey school and may actually have been in charge of all the studies there, with the title of *Lehrmeisterin.*

The name of the nun who held this office is recorded as Mechtild von Wippra. As noted earlier, the barons of Hackeborn were also lords of Wippra, and a member of the family might use either or both names. Philip Strauch, however, has pointed out that Mechtild von Hackeborn died in 1299, while a Mechtild von Wippra was still living in 1303. This seems conclusive evidence against their identification. It is likely, therefore, that Mechtild von Wippra may have been one of the cousins or nieces whose presence in the community has already been conjectured.

Whatever her title in the school it is clear that Mechtild was a teacher. Like Gertrude she often made use of comparisons drawn from academic situations. Both saints likewise called upon Christ as "best of teachers." Moreover, Christ himself designated her as a teacher when he said to Mechtild: "I entrust to you the simple and innocent children symbolized by the lamb; you are to teach them, preparing them to know and to love me."

According to some writers, Mechtild was also mistress of novices. There is no such statement, however, in the primary sources of Helfta, her own writings, or those of St. Gertrude. As official chantress and director of the choir, nevertheless, her position would have brought Mechtild into close contact with the novices.

In fact, it is as a singer and choir mistress that Mechtild is most often designated. The title, *Domna Cantrix,* "Lady Chantress," distinguishes her from the other members of the community. As choir mistress, it was Mechtild's duty to instruct the novices in the ceremonies of the choral office and to assist them in memorizing the long liturgical texts. Dom David Knowles has pointed out the practical reason for the memorization; "Until the fourteenth century," he says, "the choir was in darkness save for candles on the lectern, except on great feasts; it was, therefore, essential that the monks should know by heart not only the whole psalter with the customary canticles and hymns, but the versicles also, the anthems, and the whole of the 'common' office of saints."[1]

For forty years Mechtild's rich voice led the chant of the nuns, intoning the psalms of the Divine Office and supervising the choir. Passage after passage in the *Book of Special Grace* refers to her role as musician, "the nightingale of Christ." She repeatedly hails her Lord as *"Cantor cantorum."*

A SECRET SHARED

Although God had manifested himself to Mechtild from her earliest youth, she had told no one about these communications until, at the divine command, she broke her long silence. St. Gertrude was her confidant. Even to her she did not tell everything, but only what she believed would be to God's glory and the good of others. These confidences were sometimes interrupted, especially during her illnesses. Often Mechtild would come to a stop, un-

[1] David Knowles. *The Religious Orders in England* (Cambridge, 1948) p. 285.

able to find words for her experiences. At times her voice was so low that her friend could not hear her perfectly.

It is noteworthy that St. Mechtild never sought these spiritual favors. More than once it is recorded she was in anguish lest it were her own imagination rather than the voice of God that she heard interiorly.[2]

Not until Mechtild was fifty was the record of her life begun by order of the Abbess Sophia (successor to the Abbess Gertrude) and of a "prelate"—perhaps the provost of the monastery or the Bishop of Halberstadt. This is the work known properly as *The Book of Special Grace,* and popularly, as *Revelations of St. Mechtild.*

When she learned that Gertrude and another nun had compiled a record of the great graces she had received, the saint was all but inconsolable. Only by a special revelation could she be reconciled to their action.

St. Mechtild was already in her last illness when her book was begun. Her death at fifty-seven brought great sorrow to her community, and most particularly to her closest friend, St. Gertrude. Her account of the death of "our chantress of blessed memory" relates how the Lord Jesus, *Cantor cantorum,* himself intoned the words, *"Venite, benedicti patris mei, percipite regnum"* for his "nightingale."

During her agony, St. Mechtild was heard to murmur repeatedly, "Good Jesus, good Jesus!" At the last, as the sisters approached to ask her prayers, although she could hardly speak, she immediately replied to each one.

Because of Gertrude's own weakness, she had not been able to pray for her friend during her last hours as fervently as she would have wished. Therefore, after Mechtild's death she offered special prayers in honor of the five

[2] One is reminded of St. Teresa who begged Christ to beware lest people should be deluded into believing her a holy woman.

wounds of Christ to atone for this neglect. She was consoled by a vision of flowers springing from the wounds and by hearing the voice of her dear friend acknowledging her remembrance.

Thereafter, Gertrude invoked Mechtild's help with the utmost confidence based on a new realization of her friend's great holiness and in particular of her patience during her long illness. "Never was there anyone like her in our monastery," she writes sorrowfully, "alas, I fear there will never be another."

SAINT OF THE COMMON LIFE

As a member of a well-known family which had for three generations been patrons of the community, as sister of the abbess, and as official chantress, Mechtild von Hackeborn was naturally a prominent person at Helfta. Far from presuming on her privileges, however, she was, as St. Gertrude witnesses, profoundly humble. When Christ asked her what she wished him to do for her, she answered, "The word of command does not become me."

Moreover, her respect for superiors was undiminished by the fact that her sister held the highest office in the community. Once on a Good Friday, the Lord had said to her: "I tell you the truth: whoever scorns his superiors spits in my face."

At the service of everyone in the house, Mechtild was so generally useful that it seemed, says Gertrude, as if God wished none of his gifts to her to escape notice. In addition to her natural charm and extraordinary holiness, Mechtild had a keen intelligence, a mastery of the contemporary curriculum, and a gift for writing.

Set apart by so many marks of God's favor, Mechtild nevertheless remained very much one of the sisters. Severe to herself, she never chilled others by an austere manner.

An endearing absentmindedness was well known to her friends. Once when dining with guests she remarked that she did not eat meat. As she was in the very act of making this assertion, however, one of the visitors quietly placed before her a piece of meat which she ate, serenely unconscious of her action.

St. Bernard, it is said, went to a meal "as if to torment." St. Mechtild's neighbors at table might have shared his attitude when Mechtild was so absorbed in God that she was unaware of the noisome condition of an egg she was eating. Her companions, not so enraptured, soon informed her.

Like her friend Gertrude, Mechtild lived the common life as fully as her health permitted, seeing every detail of the daily routine as a source of merit. On the feast of St. John the Evangelist when the bell rang for Matins, she saw angels with flaming torches escorting the sisters to the sanctuary. Those who had risen from their beds with love and joy *(hilariter)* received more glory than the others. At other times, when for the salvation of mankind the sisters performed the penance of taking the discipline, Mechtild heard the sound of the strokes making melody in heaven: "the holy angels dance; the demons run away; souls are delivered from suffering, and the chains of sin are broken."

Mechtild's constant prayer for her sisters was that God might sustain them in his service, multiply his blessings upon them, make them increase in virtue and prosper in every good work. On several occasions, during her visions, she took the hand of Christ and with it blessed her beloved community. When Christ assured her that he would accomplish all her desires she led him to each sister in turn that he might give his grace to her. Finding in her a model as well as a teacher, it is no wonder that, as St.

Gertrude reports, the sisters flocked about Mechtild listening to her "with all the attention they would give to a preacher."

TEACHER, COUNSELOR, AND FRIEND

Having struggled with distractions herself, Mechtild could pray with sincere fervor for the nun who complained of wandering thoughts and lack of devotion at office. It is amusing to read that once the saint could not remember whether she had said Compline on the day before. Acknowledging her negligence with shame, she recited the omitted prayers and then made her usual preparation for communion. Later, still in doubt, she appealed to the Blessed Virgin—had she or had she not really forgotten to say Compline on the previous day? "If you do not know," answered our Lady, "that amounts to the same thing as having forgotten to say it."

In her diagnosis of spiritual maladies, Mechtild made use of the instruction she had received from Christ: "Some timid souls are afraid to entrust themselves to my tenderness, and in their fright try to flee from my face; they have a trembling paralysis. Some are flighty and inconstant; thoughts run helter-skelter through their minds; a single word is enough to make them impatient or angry. Others have a sleeping paralysis; they do everything languidly and halfheartedly." Mechtild taught that meditation on the Passion of Christ is the remedy for all these ailments.

In preparation for the second Sunday after Epiphany when the image of the Holy Face was venerated at Rome, Mechtild urged the sisters to make a spiritual pilgrimage by reciting as many Our Fathers as there were miles between Helfta and Rome. She also composed a prayer in honor of the Holy Face, one of many which she dictated, "so many" says St. Gertrude, "that if they were gathered into one volume, it would be larger than the psalter." (St. Mechtild's prayers to the Sacred Heart were favorites of St. Peter Canisius. He copied some of them into a little book which he kept with him always, even on his death-bed.)

The compilers of *The Book of Special Grace* believed that the great graces received by Mechtild "were given not so much for herself as for us and for those who will come after us." That the saint herself shared this view is clear; she often transmitted to others some precept she had received from Christ. The following examples are representative of her practical counsels:

> When children have reached the age of twelve, they should be taught what is right and their faults should be earnestly corrected. If this were done, there would not be so many lost in religious life and on the ways of virtue.
>
> If any obstacle arises in our service of God, whether from the attitude of others, from external circumstances, from our own desires, memories, or from any other cause—whatever the impediment, we should take it as a messenger from God, sending it back to him, so to speak, with praise and thanksgiving.
>
> Three things very pleasing to God are: first, never to abandon one's neighbor in his needs, and to excuse his shortcomings and sins as much as possible; second, in tribulation to seek refuge only in God, abandoning to him alone all that disquiets the heart; third, to walk with him in truth.
>
> When it is time to eat or to sleep, say in your heart: "Lord, in union with the love with which you created this useful thing for me, and yourself made use of it when you were on earth, I take it for your eternal praise and for my bodily need."
>
> The Blessed Virgin tells us: "If you wish to be truly holy, stay close to my Son; he is holiness itself, making all things holy."
>
> We should be lovingly grateful not only for the spiritual blessings God gives us, but for all bodily necessaries, such

as food and clothing, receiving them with a sincerely thankful heart and considering ourselves unworthy of them. We should also thank God for everything that he has given to his Mother and to the angels.

As the Child Jesus frequently looked at his hands, foreseeing the wounds of the nails, so we should often anticipate death and things to come.

Works which give no human satisfaction may nevertheless be very pleasing to God.

What best pleases God in members of religious orders is purity of heart, holy desires, gentle kindness in conversation, and works of charity.

When you are alone, raise your heart constantly to God, speak with him, and direct all your desires to him with great intensity. You can never be in so large a crowd that you are not alone with him.

When a man receives from his lord the gift of a fine orchard, he cannot taste the fruit until it is ripe. Likewise, when one receives a special grace, he does not experience any interior joy until by the practice of mortification he has broken the hard rind of earthly pleasure.

In an extended precept, Mechtild tells how the soul may attain to God by consecration of the bodily senses. Christ had said to her: "Seek me through your five senses, just as a host awaiting the arrival of a very dear friend looks through the doors and windows to see if the expected guest is coming. The faithful soul ought to watch for me unceasingly through the senses which are the windows of the spirit. If he sees beautiful or lovable things, let him think how beautiful, lovable, and good is the one who made them. When he hears an enchanting melody or an excellent discourse, let him say to himself: 'O how sweet will be the voice that will one day call me!' And when he hears conversation or something read aloud, let him seek his Beloved therein."

The secret of the sweetness which attracted so many persons to Mechtild may be learned from one of the coun-

sels given to her by Christ at the Introit of the mass . . .
Ego cogito . . . "I think thoughts of peace and not of
affliction." He said to her: "If you wish to be very dear
and like unto me, imitate me in these words. For as I think
the thoughts of peace and not of affliction, so do you ever
strive to have a quiet heart and peaceful thoughts, not contending with anyone, but patiently, humbly, sweetly conversing with all. So also, as I hearken unto all who call
upon me, do you show yourself easy of bearing and of
kindly will in all things; strive, moreover, to bring all out
of their captivity; that is, to bestow help and comfort upon
all who are in trouble and temptation."

St. Mechtild's devotion to her companions did not end
with their deaths. Once she recognized among the sisters
in the choir a friend of hers who had recently died. "Tell
me," Mechtild asked her, "is everything in the next life just
as I told you it would be?" "Yes," answered her friend,
"all that you said is perfectly true, and now I have found
my hundredfold."

Not only her fellow-nuns but also many persons outside
her community sought Mechtild's advice and friendship.
That some of these visitors were her relatives may be conjectured from a question that she put to Christ: "Did you,
after the return from Egypt to Nazareth, maintain relations
with your family?" "How else," he answered, "could the
scriptures have said 'They (Mary and Joseph) sought him
among their relatives and friends?' "

The extent of Mechtild's apostolate outside her own
community may be judged from a number of passages in
The Book of Special Grace. She is reported to have prayed
for "an ill-tempered man of religion" and for another
"who thought himself wiser than his superiors." (Despite
his fault, however, this person, she learned, merited a
special reward after his death because he had served mass

devoutly.) Some of the Friars Preachers also consulted her when they were harassed by temptations. She encouraged one by a forceful comparison: "Those temptations cannot hurt you any more than gnats can destroy a mountain."

That many persons came great distances to consult her in unsettled times when travel was unsafe gives some indication of Mechtild's influence. In spite of her best efforts she was not able entirely to conceal her wonderful graces. Once when the force of divine love overcame her, says Gertrude, "even guests and strangers became aware of the heavenly intoxication she had so long kept hidden." With the sure instinct which has compelled the faithful of all times to attach themselves to those in whom God is notably present, they asked her prayers and were not astounded when she was able to read their hearts. These persons deserved the reward which, as Mechtild says, is due to those who revere the gifts of God in others.

Evidently the saint sometimes corresponded with persons who asked her help. In a letter to a laywoman she employs military terms with a vigor and assurance that remind us that her name, Mechtild, means "strength in battle." She writes: "Ask of the Savior armies to strengthen you for victory against the assault of vices. If thieving wicked thoughts try to take you by surprise, run to the arsenal and there clothe yourself with the ever-shining armor of your Savior's Passion and death."

It is often related of Mechtild that after receiving some great grace she would pray that the same grace might be given to one of her friends. A passage in the *Book of Special Grace* gives the impression that Mechtild had at least four close friends. St. Gertrude was her special confidant. Another unnamed nun who assisted Gertrude in the compilation of the *Book of Special Grace* was also an intimate companion. After Mechtild's death, another account relates, two of her friends in thanksgiving for the divine favors Mechtild had received, undertook to recite an anthem for each day of her life. Another friend arranged to have a mass said for each year of the saint's life.

It was probably Gertrude who, after Mechtild's death, asked her to obtain for each of her friends whatever grace was lacking to her. "In the light of eternal truth," the saint answered, "I now see clearly that all my love for those who were dear to me in life is no more than a drop in the ocean in comparison with the love of the Sacred Heart for them. I see also why God permits persons to keep certain faults which humiliate and discipline them on the way of salvation. I would not wish to change by one iota what the omnipotent wisdom and mercy of my kind Savior has planned for each one. I can only praise and thank him."

"DOMNA CANTRIX"

Jean Leclercq has noted that in the Cistercians' preface to their reformed antiphonary, "ideas on musical technique were adapted to spiritual considerations."[3] Similarly, for Mechtild music was not only a bridge between heaven and earth; it was the meeting place for all the members of the Mystical Body. When she intoned an anthem, the angels continued it; when a virgin entered heaven, Mechtild heard her steps resounding melodiously; she declared that the sweet voice of Christ will be the eternal reward of those who close their ears to useless and dangerous words. One night "when she could not sleep for sorrow," the saint heard the angels singing, "Cast thy care upon the Lord and he will sustain thee."

It has been said of Mechtild, "She became a mystic

[3] Jean Leclercq, *The Love of Learning and the Desire for God* (New York, 1960) p. 301.

through the divine office and her musical gifts." During the chanting of the office and at mass, her devotion was so intense that the other nuns were moved to similar fervor. Many of her greatest graces came to her while she recited the psalms. Wholly absorbed in the meaning of the words, she obeyed the injunction of St. Augustine: "Meditate in your heart on that which you utter with your voice." As she conformed to the rubric which directs that the chantress should incline her head after intoning an antiphon, Christ told her, "You are bowing under the outpouring of grace and expressing praise and thanksgiving." Her sisters could learn from her how to say the office well: at the beginning of each hour, they were to bow in homage to the humility which impelled the Son of God to descend from heaven in becoming man; during the chanting of the psalms, they were to honor his infinite wisdom in teaching man through the prophets, through the words of the saints, and through his own instructions. At the conclusion of each hour they were to give thanks for all that Christ did and suffered for men, especially in whatever mystery of his life was commemorated by that hour of the office.

Once during Advent, Mechtild saw the Lord standing in the middle of the choir while from his face "more radiant than a thousand suns" came rays which illuminated all the sisters. Again, when she was praying for her community, she heard the Blessed Virgin herself intone the hymn, *"Jesu corona virginum,"* and from the air the voices of saints and angels continued with the line, *"Te laudamus in saeculum."* As she bowed when reciting the Gloria Patri, Mechtild once saw the Virgin Mary opposite her, bowing likewise in the most reverent manner, "with more reverence than any other creature." It is no wonder that sometimes the saint would extend her hands or lift them up, completely unconscious of what she was doing.

Mechtild's glorious singing was not without its cost. Sometimes it seemed to her in her fatigue and exhaustion that she could no longer draw her breath, yet she continued to sing with such fervor that she would not have stopped even if the effort were to cost her life. On several occasions she was overcome by the realization of God's love for her, and had to be assisted from the choir. At other times his visible presence sustained and enabled her to continue the chant. She seemed then to be singing "in and with God."

Like St. Gertrude, she loved the responsory *Regnum Mundi;* after her death, the sisters heard Mechtild's beautiful voice joining theirs as they sang it. On the feast of St. Catherine of Alexandria, about five weeks after the death of the *Domna Cantrix,* Gertrude saw her in company with Christ, "directing the chant according to her custom." "When I chanted with you in choir, I desired to raise your thoughts to God as the notes ascended, and to draw down his graces upon you with the descending notes. That is what I am still doing," she told her wondering friend. During another mass celebrated after Mechtild's death, Gertrude again saw her, clothed in luminous crystal garments which gave forth an exquisite melody resounding throughout heaven.

Because for St. Mechtild, music was the chief means of praising God, she was in anguish whenever it was perverted or misused. When during the carnival season before Lent she heard the people singing lascivious songs, she was so grieved *(zelo Dei et compassionis affectu nimium inardescens)* that to make reparation, she strewed broken glass and sharp instruments on her bed. This is the most severe penance recorded in her life.

Perhaps some of the songs she heard on this occasion were similar to the famous *Carmina Burana.* The collection belongs to the thirteenth century, but many of the pieces are from earlier times. Although some are extremely beautiful, the singers of others are described by Peter of Blois as *"illicitos amores canere et se corruptorem virginum iactitare."* According to Raby, a modern critic, certain of the songs are "of an unmatched obscenity."

CONSOLER AND ALLY

It was not only with her music that Mechtild contributed to the welfare of her community. She also helped her sister, the abbess, in both spiritual and temporal affairs with wisdom and efficiency, St. Gertrude testifies. As noted previously, her devotion to all the nuns, particularly those who were suffering, made Mechtild their counselor and consoler. She was a true mother to them "so that everyone who approached her came away either comforted or enlightened." Being so greatly loved and so frequently consulted must sometimes have been wearying. Gertrude, who had the same experience, candidly remarks, "Everyone loved her and wanted to be with her, and in the end this was a great burden." Sisters who suffered from scruples, who found it hard to obey their superiors, who were overwhelmed by their duties—all fled to Mechtild for advice and relief. Generously she obeyed the precept, "Bear ye one another's burdens."

In delicate health herself, Mechtild once feared that she had been guilty of imprudence in serving someone. Christ appeared to her holding the garments of the person she had been helping, and preparing to mend them himself. "Do not be afraid," he said. "Everything you do for her is done for me." Mechtild took it as a special sign of God's favor that she had much to suffer from this individual.

Again, as Mechtild prayed for a woman burdened with heavy menial labors, she saw her kneeling in prayer before Christ while he poured upon her uplifted hands a healing balm from his own. "Look," he said, "I am giving you all my works to sanctify yours and to supply what is lacking in them." Mechtild understood from this vision that the labors of this person (perhaps one of the nuns) were extremely pleasing to God. After telling the saint what prayers the hardworking woman should say when work left no time for extended meditations, Christ added, "Tell her to try to answer everyone gently."

Seeing a few sisters sleepy and distracted during mass, Mechtild exclaimed, "O my Savior, how weak and miserable we human beings are since we cannot keep awake even during the sacred mysteries!" Christ replied, "It is not hard to keep awake if one thinks of the joys of heaven or of the pains of hell." "But if some cannot—?" she insisted. "Whoever has a beloved friend," he answered, "grieves at being deprived of his presence. If one realized that I am an infinitely loving and faithful friend, ready to share with whomever comes to me those secrets which can fully satisfy her desire, one would be eager to find all delight in me. If one realized the joy of heart, the power, the liberty that I have to give, she would certainly not sleep."

With sympathetic alertness, Mechtild interceded for sisters who were suffering. Once she saw the nuns laying their grievances and burdens like green leaves upon the cross of Christ. He graciously accepted them, and with great patience and joy carried them, while all the nuns helped him.

To a sister who was discouraged she brought this message from Christ: "Why is she troubled? I created her for myself; I have given myself to her for the fulfillment of all her desires. I am her father by creation, her mother by redemption, her brother in the sharing of my kingdom, her sister by sweet companionship."

More than once, as she watched the community go to the altar to receive the sacrament, Mechtild saw each sister holding a lamp whose brilliance illumined her face. She understood that these lamps symbolized the sisters' hearts burning with the love of God. (In a letter to her young niece, Nanna, St. Catherine of Siena makes use of a similar comparison.)

The novices were especially dear to Mechtild, and she often asked Christ to make them holy and faithful. "Let them pray often and devoutly," he said to her, "read and hear scripture willingly, apply themselves to study, obey the rule carefully, preserve humility above all things without comparing themselves to others, and never look down on anyone. If they pray as I wish, I shall teach them my Divine Will and everything they need to know. While they read, I shall make them taste my sweetness; I shall sanctify them while they work; for their obedience to the rule I shall give them my compassion, my strength, and my help. In their humility I shall find my repose." This wise and precise instruction was reinforced by an appealing comparison which Mechtild had learned from the Mother of God: "One who wishes to be united to my Son ought to conduct herself like a young noblewoman espoused to a man whose rank is much higher than hers. For fear of dishonoring or displeasing him, she will be most careful to observe all the rules of etiquette. Likewise the soul belonging to God will avoid the smallest sin; she will seek consolation in him alone; and if he does not grant it immediately, she will suffer patiently like a loyal wife who does not wish to be consoled by anyone but her husband."

MECHTILD'S SPIRITUALITY

The keynote of Mechtild's spirituality, the source of her ceaseless praise of God, is renewal, purification, and the confidence they inspire.

This same confidence marked St. Mechtild's attitude toward the Holy Eucharist. An earnest advocate of frequent communion, she also urged the nuns to be generous in praying for others when they were sacramentally united to Christ. "One should be as liberal as a queen at the king's table," she would say. "He is pleased when we confidently expect great things of him." Again she said, "He never wearies even if we entreat him a thousand times a day."

Once on an Easter morning, desiring to participate fully in all the devotions of the community, Mechtild walked in the procession even though she was so weak that she had to use a staff. As she did so, she saw Christ beside her, carrying a crimson banner.

In another passage, the staff is the subject of a spiritual interpretation. When Mechtild was grieving over her faults, Christ appeared as her advocate before his Father. To support her, he gave her a staff which signified his human nature. To her surprise she saw that it had no knob at the top to rest her hand. Christ said: "I shall put my own hand there to sustain you. From now on, whenever I give you relief in your sadness, remember that you are sustained by me; but when you feel no consolation, know that I have withdrawn my hand. At such times you must cling to me with all the fidelity of your heart."

"What do you do, Lord, when I pray or recite psalms?" Mechtild once asked. "I listen," he answered. "When you work, I rest, and the more zealously you labor the more sweetly I repose in you . . . when you sleep, I watch and guard you."

48

Among the many humble requests for instruction which she addressed to Christ, her "best of teachers," one question was, what was his greatest suffering on Calvary. She was told that it was being stretched upon the cross so that all his members were dislocated. (This agony is mentioned more than once in *The Book of Special Grace.*) Another time she asked in what manner the Son of God offered praise to his Father and learned that it was by the one word *fiat.*

In addition to these, she asked a number of other questions, some of which may seem quaint to a modern reader: "My Lady, why were you without a bed and the other things that would have been useful to you?" Mechtild asked the Blessed Virgin during the Christmas season. "Nothing of that sort was necessary," was the answer. "I brought forth my innocent child without any pain."—"But when your relatives and friends came to visit you, although you were queen of heaven, what could you offer them, O poorest of ladies?" she inquired. "They had no need of my provisions; on the contrary, they brought me what I needed." was the reply.

One of the questions Mechtild asked shows her curiosity about a topic of special interest to the medieval mind. "At the request of a friar, she had asked the Savior where were the souls of Solomon, of Samson, of Origen, and of Trajan. He replied: "I wish that the dispositions of my mercy toward the soul of Solomon should remain hidden from men so that they may most carefully avoid the sins of the flesh. What my kindness has done for the soul of Samson will also remain unknown so that men may be afraid to take vengeance on their enemies. What I have done for Origen will likewise be concealed so that no one may exalt himself, relying on his knowledge. Finally, what my generosity has provided for Trajan must by my will be unknown to men in order that the Catholic faith may be the more extolled, for that emperor, although endowed with all virtues, had neither Christian faith nor baptism." (After the reference to Origen, someone has added a marginal note in the St. Gall manuscript of the *Book of Special Grace:* "What my kindness has done for the soul of Aristotle will remain hidden lest the philosopher limit himself to nature and despise celestial and supernatural things."[4])

In comparing the mystical experiences of St. Mechtild with other saints one may note several resemblances. For example, like St. Catherine of Siena, Mechtild was directed to make a dwelling for Christ within her heart; this was to have but one window through which he might speak and distribute his gifts to others. By this image she was taught to use her speech only for God's interests. One is likewise reminded of St. Teresa of Avila when reading that during a procession in honor of the Ascension, while the nuns were singing *"Et benedixit eis,"* Mechtild saw in the air above the abbey a hand of inexpressible beauty blessing the community. St. Teresa also once had a similarly beautiful vision of the hand of Christ.

In her spirituality, St. Mechtild also anticipates St. John Eudes' devotion to the Immaculate Heart of Mary from which she once saw two rays of light coming forth and illuminating the two sides of the choir. She was then inspired to greet the holy heart of Mary in honor of the seven occasions when the Blessed Virgin had particularly benefited mankind: first, when she desired the birth of her Son with a desire which went far beyond that of the patriarchs and prophets; second, when her ardent and humble love made her fit to be the Mother of God; third, when she gently and lovingly reared the child Jesus;

---

[4] The same inquiry and a similar answer are found in the visions of Elizabeth of Schonau (+1164).

fourth, when she preserved his words with diligence; fifth, when she imitated the patience of Christ in his sufferings; sixth, when she prayed for and desired the welfare of the new-born Church; finally, for what she accomplishes daily in heaven when she seconds our prayers in the presence of the Blessed Trinity.

UNION IN DESOLATION

The reader should not visualize St. Mechtild's life as untroubled and serene, one spent in a peaceful conventual round of work and prayer, and made interesting by the receiving and transmitting of messages from heaven. This saint had much to suffer in mind and body. For example, her violent headaches sometimes lasted for weeks. Moreover, she was often sleepless. In her later years, Mechtild suffered from the stone and, like St. Gertrude, had some form of hepatitis. Her final illness lasted three years.

Because she seems a somewhat gentler, perhaps more restrained person than her younger friend, St. Gertrude, it is with some astonishment that one reads of her behavior during a long illness made more trying by the withdrawal of the sense of Christ's presence. She lamented this deprivation so bitterly that her cries were heard throughout the house.

St. Mechtild also suffered much mental pain from a variety of causes: the recollection of her faults; her inability to attend community exercises or perform her usual devotions when she was ill; the conviction that her sickness made her useless; and her grief over "her wasted life and graces." Sometimes the reason for the disquietude which made her sleepless is not specified.

Not the least of her sufferings was the fright and sadness caused by diabolical temptations. At such times Mechtild wondered whether her spiritual communications and special graces were really from God. Overwhelmed and depressed, she threw herself at the feet of Christ who, calling her by name, reassured her, reminding her that the devil had dared to tempt him even when he was hanging on the cross.

The physical and mental suffering of Mechtild's last years is not incompatible with her mystical union. On the contrary, it underlines the paradox of the union and desolation of the crucified Christ. Not content with offering her involuntary sufferings in expiation for her sins and those of others, Mechtild sought other mortifications. Her self-denial at meals has already been mentioned. St. Gertrude tells us that she also had fewer and worse garments than the other sisters; her habit was worn and patched, and she had only one veil. The abbess, with her usual kindness to the sick, sometimes ordered her to sleep after Matins. When she had scarcely recovered from illness, however, Mechtild resumed her spiritual exercises.

In all her penances the saint was mindful of the many outrages committed against God by members of the Church: clergymen who neglected the study of Scripture or made use of it only for show; "spiritual persons" who disregarded the interior life and gave themselves to external works; the common people who cared neither for the word of God nor for the sacraments.

What were the sins for which Mechtild punished herself so sharply? Gertrude knows of only one—in her childhood Mechtild had falsely asserted that she saw a thief in the courtyard. She regarded this as a serious offense. Among her self-accusations Mechtild also includes speaking ill of someone and of "inopportune silence."

Once after she had made a general confession, the priest told her to recite the *Te Deum*. After her death and that of her sister, the abbess Gertrude, two confessors testified that they had never encountered souls more innocent. (This statement is quoted in the *Liber Specialis Gratiae.* The fact that St. Gertrude is not included in the commendation is taken as one of the internal evidences of her authorship.)

That Mechtild was occasionally scandalized, that she could become indignant at a display of ill-temper, that she found it hard to be waited on when she was ill, that she was afraid of death—these are encouraging reminders that with all her spiritual gifts, she remained a member of the human race. True, she had the unwavering will essential to holiness, but her tact and understanding of individual differences kept her from rigidity in her dealings with others. In a charming comparison, Mechtild recognizes three among the many types of souls: the nightingales who are enamored of God; the larks, who perform their good works with joyous humility; and the doves, simple souls who quietly receive the gifts of God without discussing his doings nor those of men.

The Book of Special Grace

It has already been noted that St. Mechtild was at first greatly distressed when she learned that St. Gertrude and another nun had compiled the *Book of Special Grace.* Soon afterward, however, she had a vision of Christ holding the volume. He said to her, "All this has been committed to writing by my will and inspiration; and therefore you have no cause to be troubled about it." He also reminded her that as he had been liberal in his graces to her, she should likewise be generous in sharing them. The title of the work, *Book of Special Grace,* was to signify not simply that Mechtild herself had received special grace, but that reading about her experiences would be an occasion of special grace to others. (The compilers of the book also were assured that Christ himself had assisted them.)

Once St. Mechtild was convinced that the volume had been written according to God's will, she was no longer disturbed, but willingly read and corrected it. Thereafter she was as little concerned as if it had been written about another person.

THE AUTHORS

The actual writing of the *Book of Special Grace* is the work of two nuns, one of whom was certainly St. Gertrude. Evidence for this conclusion may be found in the fact that a number of passages deal with episodes recorded also in *The Herald of Divine Love.* The fact that Gertrude's name is never mentioned in the *Book of Special Grace* is also circumstantial evidence of her authorship. Such expressions as "the person to whom she told these things" or "another sister had the same experience" indicate Gertrude's identity. Most convincing of all is the style of certain chapters, notably Chapter 30 in Book Five which gives a summary account of Mechtild's life and virtues. The fluid, clear, and graceful Latin is so similar to that of Book Two of the *Herald,* admittedly by Gertrude, that the Solesmes editors of both books have no doubt of their common authorship. A number of footnotes throughout their edition add to the evidence for Gertrude's composition.

That St. Gertrude wrote her original works in Latin is clear from several passages in both *The Book of Special Grace* and in the *Herald of Divine Love.* In the *Herald,* for example, the word *mansuetudo* is analyzed and interpreted. In the *Book of Special Grace,* Gertrude refers to a Latin word she is using, *ovum,* as having two syllables. A few German words are also used in the latter work, always in a colloquial context; for instance, *minne* (love).

DIVISIONS OF THE WORK

The Book of Special Grace has seven divisions. The first begins with a consideration of the Annunciation and Incarnation and concludes with the feast of the Dedication of a Church. Throughout this section there are many suggestions for honoring Christ, his Mother, and the saints on their feasts. These are followed by a little treatise on the Blessed Virgin.

The second division of the book, in which many of St. Mechtild's experiences are narrated, deals with the intimate relations of the soul with God. The third and fourth sections are similar in content, but treat more specifically of some circumstances of conventual life. The fifth part deals with the after-life and refers to a number of persons known to the community at Helfta: the Abbess Gertrude, the former beguine Mechtild von Magdeburg, some Dominican friars, and a little girl named Orlamunde.

Of the last named, the account tells us that before her birth she was consecrated to God by her mother. Although she died in childhood, the girl received in heaven the reward of one who had belonged to a religious order, just as an infant who dies after baptism is saved by the faith of his godparents. (Mechtild adds that Orlamunde was so beautiful that had she grown to maturity, her father would have insisted on her remaining in the world.) The sixth and seventh books of this work tell of the life, death, and heavenly reward of the Abbess Gertrude and of St. Mechtild.

Simply to list the themes of the *Book of Special Grace* would give the reader no idea of the dynamism, color, and charm of St. Mechtild's book. There is nothing static about her descriptions—all is alive, moving, changing, and shining. She has the eye of a painter and the fresh mind of a child.

Dr. Wilhelm Oehl lists the following as subjects common to the literature of mysticism: meditation on the birth, sufferings, and death of Christ, mystical love, mystical intoxication, the dance of the soul, the spiritual battle for salvation, eschatology, the symbolism of numbers, criticism of the times, and the theological and symbolic use (derived from antiquity and beloved by the Middle Ages) of zoology, botany, and mineralogy. In its inclusion of these themes, *The Book of Special Grace* is representative of the literature of medieval mysticism.

THE USE OF SYMBOLISM

It has been said that the function of the symbol is to reveal "certain aspects of reality . . . which defy all other modes of knowledge." Mechtild's figurative use of flowers, animals and landscapes may be illustrated by the following examples. In her writings, the lily ordinarily represents innocence; the violet and crocus humility; herb bennet, thanksgiving. The rose, the flower most often used in Mechtild's comparisons, is mentioned at least five times as the symbol of patience. (This association is not original with Mechtild. To give only one instance of its occurrence elsewhere, a traditional hymn in honor of St. Dominic hails him as *rosa patientiae. Geduld bringt Rosen* says the proverb.) In other passages Mechtild employs this flower to symbolize charity, love of God's will, martyrdom, prayer, and the heart of Mary. A five-petaled rose is the symbol for Our Lady's five senses—St. Mechtild calls her the rose without thorns. In a vision of Christ suffering, he is described as "the rose without thorns yet wounded by thorns." A beautiful image, that of a green rose, symbolizes the confidence in God shown by the Abbess Gertrude.

To the graphic mind of the Middle Ages, animals frequently symbolized virtues and vices. For Mechtild, true child of her time, they often represent sinners: the lion stands for the proud, the ostrich for the hard-hearted. Hell is filled with serpents, toads, lions, dogs, and other animals.

In the hearts of sinners she sees monsters symbolizing a gnawing conscience. These creatures are worms with the heads and paws of dogs and long tails. Christ is represented by the lamb and the bee. Sheep and lambs usually represent souls, Mechtild's among them. Her soul is also said to be like a hare "asleep with its eyes open"; this is her version of the line, "I sleep and my heart watches." She says also that one should be like a trusty little dog who always returns to its master even after frequent rebuffs. If one is wounded by a word, she should not withdraw; or if she does so, she should return at once, relying on God's mercy which, for a single sigh, pardons everything.

The ant figures in a striking comparison. When Mechtild was overwhelmed by God's revelation of himself to her, which came "like an impetuous torrent," she said to him: "Though you come to fulfill me wholly and enlighten me marvelously, I am nevertheless so tiny a creature that all I know and can make others know about you is no more than an ant can carry away from a vast mountain. (Mechtild von Magdeburg, the ex-beguine, it will be recalled, used similar language, but her examples were a bee and a jar of honey.)

In St. Mechtild's imagery, birds in general represent angels, while black birds are demons and temptations. Doves and eagles are frequently mentioned, the former symbolizing the Holy Spirit, the souls of the dead, simple souls, and various individuals. Eagles, in addition to representing the Holy Spirit, are symbols of Christ and of contemplative souls, notably the Abbess Gertrude. The prayers of the community appear under the form of larks.

It will be remembered that for St. Mechtild nightingales, larks, and doves also represent three types of persons pleasing to God. Her own soul is shown under the form of a bird with three wings: red for desire, green for love, yellow for hope. (A Middle English poem, "The Bird with Four Feathers" equates them with youth, beauty, strength, and wealth.)

Richly colored symbolic garments adorned with jewels and golden ornaments often figure in Mechtild's descriptions of her heavenly visitants. The liturgical colors, red, green, white and purple are most commonly used. From a number of vivid accounts, the following may be taken as typical: "The King of glory once appeared in indescribable splendor in the fulness of his joy, wearing a golden robe embroidered with doves and covered by a red mantle. This garment was open on two sides to indicate that the soul has free access to God. The red mantle symbolized the Passion. . . . The doves represented the simplicity of the divine Heart, whose dispositions are unchangeable although the creature so often fails in fidelity to him." When the Blessed Virgin appeared with the Christchild, she wore a garment woven of silver sprinkled with golden roses. The Child was in a green and white tunic covered with red and green roses. On another occasion the Blessed Virgin came "in a gown the color of air, sewn all over with tiny flowers of gold and embroidered around the neck and sleeves with the monogram of Christ." Again, she comes in a pale green cloak latticed over with gold, with the head of Christ in every lattice. St. Catherine of Alexandria is in dull crimson covered over with gold embroidery of little wheels, fastened at the breast with a clasp of two golden hands.

The exquisite minuteness of these descriptions with their effect of jeweled needlework is balanced by larger pictures in the landscapes of Mechtild's book. Since both she and Gertrude loved beautiful scenery, it is not strange that some of Mechtild's revelations are communicated in terms of enchanting vistas.

SPECTACLE

Pageantry and spectacle of the most splendid description also brighten the pages of *The Book of Special Grace.* Feasts and processions, the throne of God and the entourage of angels in the New Jerusalem, the brilliant mansions of the saints, all are witness to a conception of spiritual magnificence that recalls the paintings of Fra Angelico and the poetry of Dante. Take, for example, this scene: The saint, ascending the mountain of virtue with Christ, comes to a beautiful little silver house, transparent as crystal. Around it, white-robed children are playing delightedly and praising God. These are the souls of children who died before the age of five and are now in eternal happiness. Next, Mechtild sees a mansion of red carved stones surrounded by a singing throng dressed in purple. These are people who were married or widowed. The third house is of sapphire for an innumerable crowd of scarlet-clad saints. These are the ones who battled valiantly for Christ against the devil. The last house, of pure gold, is the dwelling-place of charity where Christ and his mother hold court.

Some other passages of remarkable interest ought to be mentioned. The first recounts St. Mechtild's interview with "the least saint in heaven." He was a man clothed in a green dress "and his hair was crisp and silvery and he was of moderate stature, exceeding fair in face and very beautiful." He said to her, "On earth I was a robber and malefactor; I never did any good action." In amazement she asked him, "How is it that you have entered into joy?" "All my evil deeds were done out of ignorance," he told her. "I had been reared in wickedness by my parents and knew no better. At the last moment by the mercy of God

I repented, and after a long time of suffering, by the gratuitous kindness of God I was led hither to the place of repose."

Another extended passage recalls in terms of a wedding festival the sufferings of Christ in his Passion: ". . . Thou canst call to mind my divine love, which drew me down from my Father's bosom and caused me to serve thirty and three years in seeking after thee. And when the time of my nuptials was at hand, I was myself sold by my own heart's love as the price of the marriage banquet, and I gave myself for bread and flesh and drink. In like manner at the banquet I myself was the harp and the organ, by means of the sweet words of my mouth; and to joyfully entertain the guests after the manner of sports I humbled myself at the feet of my disciples. . . . Thou shalt call to mind what kind of dance I who was so exceeding fair performed after the banquet, when three times I fell upon the ground and made as it were, three such powerful bounds that all dripping with bloody sweat I shed great drops of blood. In that dance I clothed all my fellow-soldiers in three-fold garments, when I obtained for them the forgiveness of their sins, the sanctification of their souls, and my divine enlightenment. . . . Thou shalt remember the love of my humility at the kiss of the bride when the betrayer came near and kissed me, at which kiss my heart felt such strong love pass through it, that had his soul repented, I would have taken it by that kiss to be my bride. For then I joined to myself all the souls which from everlasting I had predestined to be my brides. . . . Call to mind what kind of marriage songs my ears listened to for the love of my bride when I stood before the judge and so much false witness was brought forward against me. . . . Remember how becomingly for thy love I adorned myself, when so many times I changed my vestments, for white and purple and scarlet were my vestments, and for a garland of roses I wore a crown of thorns. . . . Be mindful how I embraced thee, when I was bound to the column: there for thy sake I received upon me the darts of all thine enemies. . . . Be mindful how I entered the marriage-bed of the Cross. And as spouses give their bridal clothes to actors, so did I give my vestments to the soldiers, and my body to them who crucified me. Then I stretched out my arms by means of the cruel nails for thy sweet embrace, singing on my bed of love seven long songs of marvelous sweetness."

Some passages in the foregoing seem to echo the words of St. Ambrose: "Jesus Christ came into this world to make a leap; he was with God the Father, he came into the Virgin Mary, and from the Virgin Mary into the crib or rack. He descended into flom Jordan, he ascended upon the cross, he descended into his tomb." (This is Caxton's quaint version of the passage.) The whole concept of Christ's life as a dance of love is further developed in the English carol: "Tomorrow Shall Be My Dancing-Day"; one stanza will give some idea of its character:

> For thirty pence Judas me sold
> His covetousness to advance;
> "Mark whom I kiss, the same do hold,
> The same is he shall lead the dance."

As a final example, one may cite the chapter called "How One Can Play at Dice with Christ" which is an ingenious presentation of one of St. Mechtild's constant teachings: that we can share in the merits of the Savior and make them our own. She begins by saying that the Blessed Virgin gives her the dice to present to a person for whom she (Mechtild) has been praying. "Give them to her as from me and tell her to play with my Son. When a bridegroom casts dice with his bride, he loves to take from her in the game her rings, her jewels, the pretty ornaments she has made for herself; the bride makes no objection for she knows that everything is hers that belongs to her well-beloved." Then follows a curious exposition of the significance of the marks on the dice. One point stands for man's lowliness; he throws this into the game with Christ when he accepts scorn and contradiction and willingly endures his dependence on others. He wins what Christ possesses when he receives from him the exaltation and honor which his Father gave him in compensation for his abasements on earth. Similarly the two marks on the dice stand for man's body and soul; gambling with these by performing spiritual or corporal works for the love of God, he wins from him all the works of Christ's divinity and humanity. Three points signify the powers of the soul: memory, will, and understanding; the image of the Holy Trinity is impressed on the soul that rightly employs these powers. Four points are cast when the soul abandons itself to God in prosperity and adversity, for the present and for the future; five points when the five senses are gratified only according to God's good pleasure; six points when a man devotes the six ages of his life to the service of God. In return for these plays, he receives benefits of the creation of the four parts of the earth governed by God's power and wisdom, the five wounds of Christ with all the fruits of his Passion, and the virtues and merits of Christ's holy life upon earth.

STYLE

Not merely color and originality but great vigor of expression characterize many parts of *The Book of Special Grace*. For example, when Christ's captors advanced to take him, "He went toward them as eagerly as a mother goes to snatch her child from wolves." It is also said, apropos of St. Mechtild's great devotion to the suffering Christ, that if anyone spoke of the Passion without devotion, her face and hands became "as red as a boiled crab," *(in modum decocti cancri apparerent)*.

Many passages in the *Book of Special Grace* describe the transference of Christ's merits, his Mother's, and the saints'. Often this sharing is indicated by similarity of garments. Once Christ placed his hands over Mechtild's to signify that he gave her the merits of all his works. At another time he appeared to her in a vision as a child of five. When she asked the reason, he explained: "You are now fifty. My first year compensates for your first ten years, my second for your next decade . . . Thus all your sins are effaced, your years made holy, your entire life perfected by mine."

The Blessed Virgin is also represented as offering her own graces and good works for the benefit of others. Among the saints in whose special graces Mechtild shared is St. Agnes. On her feast, Mechtild lamented that so young a child should have loved and suffered generously for Christ, whereas she, Mechtild, after many years in religious life, had accomplished so little. At this, Christ said to St. Agnes, "Give her what you have." Mechtild then understood that God has given the saints the privilege of sharing with those who honor them and thank him for their graces all the merit that the saints have won and all that Christ has accomplished in them. She also realized that the saints receive an additional glory and happiness in heaven when the faithful on earth pay them some special honor. Such insights, besides strengthening in Mechtild the sense of the reality of the Mystical Body, also contributed to her tremendous confidence in God's mercy and accessibility. "Christ is more easily possessed than a bit of thread or straw," she said; "a single wish, a sigh, is sufficient."

Obedience is recognized as the regulating virtue in monastic life. Two striking images in Mechtild's writings dramatize its value. One of the sisters who had generously sacrificed her self-will by an act of renunciation asked the saint to present her offering to God. As she did so at mass, Mechtild saw rising from the ciborium the figure of a small child who was suddenly transformed into a young girl of marvelous beauty, personifying the Divine Will. Several persons then embraced and conversed with her; these represented the souls of those who conform their wills to the will of God. At the same time Mechtild saw an ugly little scullion in smoky black clothes, the personification of self-will, who tried to attract the attention of the obedient sisters. Some disregarded him, but others began to smile at him, to speak to him, and finally to whisper with him. The description ends with the warning that if those who follow their own inclinations do not repent and become truly obedient, they will suffer eternal poverty with self-will, "that wretched scullion." (This scene recalls St. Gertrude's vision of a "despicable creature" whom she saw attempting to make her pour the poison of vainglory into the cup offered to her by Christ.)

THE FAME OF ST. MECHTILD'S BOOK

It is not surprising that the *Book of Special Grace* had wide dissemination after Mechtild's death. The Dominicans who had known and esteemed her were most active in propagating the work. In Pre-Reformation England, too, there is some evidence that St. Mechtild was known and venerated. For example, a Carthusian psalter now at Peterhouse, Cambridge, contains a meditation on the wounds of Christ and a prayer of thanksgiving *"in revelationibus b. Matilde."* Trinity College Library, Oxford, has a Latin manuscript of the *Liber Specialis Gratiae,* and at the Bodleian there is an early fifteenth-century English translation of the first five parts of the work. In this translation, however, some passages are omitted and the title is given as "The Boke of Gostely Grace" a common misreading of *Spiritualis* for *Specialis.*

This is probably the book of "visions of Blessed Matilda" willed by Cicely, Duchess of York, to her granddaughter Bridget, a Dominican nun at Dartford. Once again, therefore, we find the recurrent association of the great saints of Helfta with the Order of St. Dominic.

DANTE AND ST. MECHTILD

According to Boccaccio, St. Mechtild's book was particularly popular in Florence where the citizens used to recite *"Le laude di Donna matelda"* before the sacred images. The work was certainly known to Dante, and some scholars have seen in the gentle nun of Helfta the original of Matelda, the smiling young girl with downcast eyes who in Canto 31 of the *Purgatorio* draws the poet through the crystal waters of Lethe.

A number of passages in the *Book of Special Grace* are strikingly similar to some of Dante's images. The most obvious are the description of the seven-terraced mount with its seven fountains in Part One, chapter 13; the melodious voice singing *"Venite, benedicti Patris mei"* in Part Two, chapter 19; and the singing of the *Asperges,* Part Two, chapter 2. Mechtild's description of Purgatory in Part Five, chapter 20, also contains some details similar to Dante's; persons who have been unfaithful to their rule and religious profession walk bowed down under crushing burdens; gluttons and drunkards are shriveled up by hunger and thirst.

With Dante's description of the three steps made of marble, purple stone, and porphyry before the gate of

Purgatory in Canto 9, one may associate Mechtild's description of three steps before the altar of God, in Part One, chapter 30. Dante's steps have been regarded as symbols of examination of conscience, contrition, and penance. Mechtild's steps are made of gold for charity, blue stone for meditation on heavenly things, and green for energy in performing actions for God's honor.

Most commentators who discuss the relationship of the *Book of Special Grace* and the *Divine Comedy,* confine themselves to a comparison of Purgatory in both works. Some parallels to Dante's Paradise should also be cited. It will be remembered that in this work when the souls of the blessed manifest themselves to him in the various spheres, Dante is told that they are not actually present there; they are really in heaven, but show themselves in lower spheres to signify their differing degrees of beatitude (IV, 28-39). So in the *Book of Special Grace* when Mechtild has a vision symbolizing the praise of the Trinity, the Savior says to her: "What you see is not taking place in heaven itself but because you see me in whom every creature is contained, you see all creatures as if they were present." This passage is found in Part Four, chapter 15. Likewise, with the line in Dante, "Near and far adds not there nor takes away (XXX, 121)," one may compare St. John's explanation to Mechtild, who is surprised to see the apostles apparently below married men who possessed the goods of this world, "We are not really farther from God, for he dwells in us, just as I wrote: 'The Word was made flesh and dwelt among us'." He added, "And you, are you farther from God because of the place you occupy?"

Another parallel worthy of note occurs in Part Six, chapter 9, where the voices of the saints singing joyously enter into a long trumpet from which sounds emerge as a single melody. This description calls to mind the famous image of the eagle, symbol of justice, in the *Paradiso* (XIX) where the many spirits composing the form of the bird speak with a single voice.

Finally, the image of the wheel and cord representing the free will of man united to the perfect will of God (Part Four, chapter 20) suggests the image of the wheel with which Dante closes his great poem:

> To the high imagination force now failed;
> But like to a wheel whose circling nothing jars
> Already on my desire and will prevailed
> The Love that moves the sun and the other stars.

After noting these resemblances between the passages in the *Book of Special Grace* and in the *Divine Comedy,* one must add that other parallels may be observed in *The Flowing Light of the Divinity* by Mechtild von Magdeburg.

In Karl Vossler's treatise, *Medieval Culture,* after mentioning the writings of St. Gertrude and the two Mechtilds, he comments: "If one considers the similarities and analogues to Dante's *Purgatorio* which these works reveal, especially in reference to his Earthly Paradise and its streams of oblivion and consolation, its successive steps of purification, etc., it is hard to resist the surmise that Dante read the *Revelationes* of these Benedictine nuns or heard of them, or even that the figure of his Matelda was created as a memorial to the two Mechtilds."

It seems reasonable to conclude that Dante, like some of his contemporaries, identified the two Mechtilds, attributing to a single writer both the books from Helfta written by women who bore the same name. Yet of the two, St. Mechtild von Hackeborn, sister of the Abbess Gertrude, and Mechtild von Magdeburg, the ex-beguine, the former seems more like Dante's Matelda than does "the weather-beaten old Sybil" as Hans Urs von Balthasar calls the ex-beguine who came to Helfta *"post multas tribulationes."*

Although some commentators see no resemblance between the dancing young girl in the Earthly Paradise and the saint whom they designate as "the austere Cistercian nun," readers of the *Book of Special Grace* will agree that the two have much in common. Remember that "everyone loved St. Mechtild and wished to be with her": she had a remarkably sweet and resonant voice; images of beautiful fields and gardens, music and dancing are frequent in her book. In fact, just as the atmosphere of her spiritual garden resembles Dante's earthly Paradise, so does the personality of "Christ's nightingale" resemble that of Dante's gracious Donna Matelda.

 *The Book of Gertrude*

From the Land of Unlikeness:
A Portrait of the Saint

THE CHILD

In the year 1261 a five-year old girl was brought to the famous monastery school of Helfta and entrusted to the care of the Abbess Gertrude von Hackeborn. The child was also named Gertrude, but of her family nothing at all is known. Her birthplace may have been Thuringia, which has been called "the center and stronghold of German sanctity," or it may have been some other, perhaps more remote or even non-Germanic, region. (Although usually associated with the German people in the present day, the name Gertrude was common in several countries throughout the Middle Ages.)

Unlike many of her companions in the cloister school Gertrude did not belong to the nobility, for she has no recorded surname and may have been of humble or even of illegitimate birth. Various passages in her writings indicate that she was an orphan. One fact only is noted: she was born on the feast of the Epiphany, January 6.

Whoever was responsible for the decision to entrust the small girl to the nuns at Helfta made a wise provision for her welfare. As Gertrude became familiar with her surroundings, everything could make her say with sincerity,

"My lot is in a goodly place . . . thou hast set my feet in a spacious land." — Like all the other children in the convent school she would have had to memorize the Psalter.

At the time of the five-year-old Gertrude's arrival, Helfta was at the height of its achievement and influence. From the days of the first abbess, Cunegunde of Halberstadt, the community had won the admiration and confidence of clergy and people. Her successor, the second abbess, Gertrude von Hackeborn, was celebrated for her intelligence and holiness. With her sister, St. Mechtild, she was to become one of the most important influences in the life of her small namesake.

LAND OF UNLIKENESS

Despite the charming landscape of Helfta, the stimulating intellectual atmosphere, and the admirable observance of conventual regulations, the convent was to become for Gertrude a *regio dissimilitudinis,* "a land of unlikeness" where she would wander unhappily until Christ himself should intervene.

The change was not sudden. The nun whose biographical account of the saint forms the first portion of the *Legatus Divinae Pietatis,* reports that Gertrude loved study and quickly outstripped her young companions. As she grew to maturity she became outstanding for eloquence both in speech and in writing. Eventually, it seems, her ardor for intellectual activities made the obligations of conventual life wearisome. Possibly it may also have caused her to look down upon her less gifted companions.

From the eager, attractive child loved by all and devoted to the studies that she mastered so easily, Gertrude little by little changed into a tense and melancholy young woman. Although accepted as a member of the community, she confesses that she was a nun in appearance only.

The change had probably been imperceptible. With all the excellent qualities recorded of Gertrude's abbess, the gift of reading the heart was evidently lacking. Moreover, the younger Gertrude's self-respect and love of decorum would have kept her from any obvious transgression, while her natural charm and courtesy would have concealed the change from any but a very acute observer. "If you [Christ] had not given me a natural aversion to evil and an attraction toward the good that I saw in my companions, I should have succumbed to every temptation without remorse as if I had been a pagan living among pagans," she writes. Pride, vainglory, and curiosity had slowly darkened the brilliant mind, and now that Gertrude had given the first place in her life to intellectual interests, she found them empty and unsatisfying. Her deviation from the monastic ideal she had professed led inevitably to anxiety and depression. In Advent of 1280 her sadness came to a climax. From this desert of her own making only the hand of Christ could lead her.

THE FIRST APPARITION

In a passage of singular beauty Gertrude records how two months later, on January 27, 1281, her Lord intervened to rescue her. Appearing to her in the form of a youth of sixteen years, he addressed her in the words of the response in the Office for Advent: "Thy salvation is at hand; why art thou consumed with grief? Hast thou no counselor, that thou art so changed by sadness?" When he had said these words, although she knew that she was in the convent dormitory, yet it seemed to her that she was in her usual corner in the chapel where she was accustomed to say her half-hearted prayers. "I shall save you and deliver you. Do not be afraid," he said. After these words she saw the gentle hand of Christ take her own right hand as if in solemn assurance. He spoke again: "You have licked the dust with my enemies and have sucked honey among thorns.[1] Now return to me and I shall make you drink from the torrent of my delights." As she listened, Gertrude saw between them a tremendous hedge so set with thorns that it seemed impossible to surmount. Incapable of approaching Christ, and overcome by longing to do so, she suddenly felt herself lifted and set beside him. It was then that in the hand which had been extended to her, she saw the sacred wounds.

THE PATH OF PERFECTION

Peace and serenity returned. She began to run along the path of perfection and to seek out what she had formerly regarded as hard and insupportable.

During the three years following the great apparition of 1281, Gertrude experienced much spiritual joy. As time passed, and she perceived that she must continue to struggle against her inclinations to impatience, vainglory, and negligence, she often refreshed herself by recollecting the special marks of love that Christ had shown her. In an eloquent comparison she says, "Although the rose is

[1] ". . . and have sucked honey among thorns."
This expression was proverbial in England as early as the twelfth century. It occurs in a homily, c. 1175:

Nis nan blisse . . . that ne beo
To bitter aboht
thet et huni ther-in
beoth licked of thornes.

It is one of the *Proverbs of Hendyng,* c. 1300: "Dere is boht the hony that is licked of the thorne."
The most explicit statement occurs in the lyric, "Worldes Blis Ne Last No Throwe":

"thu likest huni of thorn iwis
that seest thi love on worldes blis
for ful of bitternis hit is."

lovelier in the spring when it is in full bloom and fragrance, nevertheless in winter, although it is withered, it still by its sweet odor recalls its former beauty. In the same way the soul finds profound joy in remembering the favors it has received." (In the *Ascent of Mount Carmel,* St. John of the Cross has written similarly: "Though the effect of the apprehension be not so great afterwards, when it is recalled as it was on the first occasion when it was communicated, yet when it is recalled, love is renewed, and the mind is lifted up to God. . . . And thus this is a great favor for the soul on which God bestows it, for it is as though it had within itself a mine of blessings.")

In the days of spring which succeeded her winter of sadness, Gertrude recovered much that had been lost to her. Her joy in nature returned, but with a difference. One beautiful morning after Prime, she entered the court and seated herself near the fish pond formed by the clear stream which flowed down the sloping ground before emptying into the lake of Seeburg below. As in her childhood she took delight in the bright water, the leafy trees, and the birds, particularly the doves. But now she asked herself, what was missing in this lovely place? The answer was plain: a companion to share her pleasure. Since the great experience of 1281, she could imagine only Christ as the one who would satisfy all her desires. But how unworthy of him she was! If only she could return to her source like the stream she watched, bring forth fruits like these trees, fly above the passions and turmoil of the world like the birds! Then perhaps she could induce him to remain with her. All day she experienced this keen longing and in her prayer at night, suddenly the Lord's words came to mind: "If anyone love me, he will keep my word, and my Father will love him, and we will come to him and make our abode with him." At that moment, Gertrude realized that without waiting for her complete purification, Christ had indeed made his home within her. Overcome by this realization, she cried out for an ocean not of water but of blood to cleanse her for his dwelling, for a blazing furnace to consume the refuse of her heart.

To Gertrude, the divine patience which watched her fluctuating efforts to amend her life seemed more notable than the patience shown to Judas. Christ seemed grieved rather than angered by her faults. In his treatment of her he seemed, she says, desirous to spare her embarrassment. Despite her forgetfulness of him, a forgetfulness lasting sometimes for hours, sometimes for days, sometimes even for weeks, on returning to herself she always found Christ present in her heart.[2]

Only once did he withdraw himself, and that was for a period of eleven days after Gertrude had indulged in "worldly conversation." How could he endure her waywardness, she wondered once after she had yielded to impatience. In answering, Christ employed one of the "similitudes" with which he was accustomed to instruct her: he likened himself to a poor invalid who sits quietly through a storm in the hope that sunshine will return.

GERTRUDE'S APOSTOLATE

With the complete reversal of values resulting from the amazing revelation of the love of Christ, Gertrude's absorption in literature gave way to a wholehearted effort to please God. Hitherto she had, as she vigorously phrases it, given as little thought to her interior life as to the interior of her feet. In her endeavors to make up for the past, she was strengthened by the familiar presence of Christ when she received holy communion.

2 Compare St. Teresa's remark: "His Majesty is pleased to punish me only by granting me fresh favors, though for one who knows herself even that is no light punishment." (*Letters,* II, 889)

After the apparition of Christ in January, 1281, the most important change in Gertrude was in her attitude toward her studies. The early biographer writes: "From a grammarian she became a theologian." Obviously, Gertrude did not renounce her former scholarship nor her love of study, but it was now a means, not an end. She was still the student: "Teach me, O dearest Lord," was her habitual prayer. Even in her most exalted spiritual writings, Gertrude remembered her rhetoric. She had read Virgil and Augustine; their phraseology was interwoven with her own. A cultivated mind is not impaired by the knowledge that God is ineffable and that human learning is finite. Now that the motive of her intellectual labors was no longer selfish, Gertrude worked harder than before. To enlighten and comfort her sisters, she spent her time in translating, paraphrasing, and explaining the Scriptures and the writings of the Fathers. Her contemporary biographer, a nun who had known and loved her for many years, compares her to a dove carefully gathering grain for its fledglings, a comparison which recalls St. Gertrude's meditation in the courtyard. She had loved these birds "because of their liberty"; now they were the symbol of devotion as well.

Gertrude's apostolate was exercised through her teaching and example, through her prayers and through her writings. It was not, however, until 1289 that she first wrote of the tremendous experience which inaugurated her new life at Helfta when she bowed her head in submission to the mercy and wisdom of God who had, as she said, prepared so apt a remedy for her spiritual sickness. Looking back eight years later and considering what her days had been before the intervention of Christ, Gertrude was again overcome by the ingenuity of the love that had brought her to her knees more effectively than any punishment could have done.

MINOR MIRACLES

During her lifetime, no spectacular manifestations of Gertrude's sanctity were noted. On one occasion, however, her prayers brought an end to intense and unseasonable cold; on another, they caused the cessation of rain which threatened to destroy the harvest. It is also recorded that when the community was at work in the court, and the gathering clouds made them fear that they could not finish, Gertrude prayed that the storm might be deferred till the work was done. (The anonymous narrator says that she heard the saint asking God for this favor.) Her wish was granted to the letter: as soon as the task had been finished, the storm started so promptly that two or three loiterers were drenched. Once when Gertrude begged Christ to stop the high winds which were causing a great drought, he explained to her that by this hardship he was inducing certain rebellious persons to turn to him in prayer. Since he did not grant her request, he substituted a spiritual gift for the favor she had asked.

One quiet little miracle reveals the saint's gentle familiarity with her Lord. She was at work seated on a pile of hay, when her stylus slipped into it. "Lord," she exclaimed playfully *(quasi jocosa)* "there is no use in my searching for it. Please help me." Without even looking, she put her hand into the hay with as much assurance as if the stylus lay on a table before her, and instantly recovered it. (According to some translators it was a needle that she lost, but the Latin reads *stylus aut acus.* As the nuns carried tablets at their sides, a desk would not be necessary, and evidently some of their writing was done out of doors. From what we know of Gertrude's life she seems more likely to have been writing than sewing, though like St. Teresa of Avila, she did some spinning.)

THE STIGMATA

Gertrude's prayers for herself were answered with similar generosity. Not long after the first apparition of Christ in the dormitory, St. Gertrude found a prayer which appealed to her greatly: "O most merciful Lord, engrave thy wounds in my heart with thy most precious blood, that I may read in them both thy grief and thy love." She frequently repeated this petition. One day, on going to the refectory for collation, she was thinking of the prayer when she suddenly realized that it had been granted: the wounds of the Lord were imprinted on her heart. "By these wounds," she writes, "you have healed my spirit." From that time, the contemplation of the sacred wounds became one of her habitual devotions. Writers on mysticism recognize both visible and invisible stigmata. According to Poulain, "The substance of this grace consists in pity for Christ, participation in his sufferings, sorrows, and for the same end—the expiation of the sins unceasingly committed in the world." St. Gertrude is traditionally included among stigmatics.[3]

It is remarked by the saint that when this tremendous grace came to her in the refectory, she was beside someone who knew the secrets of her soul. This person was almost certainly St. Mechtild, and the proximity of the two saints at this moment seems like the blessing of Christ on their friendship. Immediately after mentioning her friend, St. Gertrude goes on to say that she has often felt an increase of fervor as a result of imparting her confidence. Yet she cannot say whether she has been led by human affection

[3] A. Poulain, "Stigmata" *Catholic Encyclopedia* (New York, 1913) XIV, 294.

or by the grace of God. She has been told, however, by an experienced person that it is good to open one's heart, not to any and all, but to those who have a faithful affection for us, who are more advanced than ourselves, and who are to be respected for their age. If she has been influenced by human love, she adds, she has cause to be still more grateful to God who has communicated his riches to her nothingness. Elsewhere, it is noted that she held most dear those who were nearest to God.

THE WOUND OF DIVINE LOVE

Seven years later, toward the end of her life, Gertrude received another privilege which was also to be given to St. Teresa of Avila. Having asked one of her friends who prayed daily before the crucifix to intercede for her that her heart might be pierced by the wound of divine love, she received a premonition of this grace on Gaudete Sunday in Advent. As she was going to holy communion, she prayed fervently that although unworthy of the wound of divine love, she might nevertheless receive it through the desires and merits of the community. While making her thanksgiving after communion, she noticed an arrow-tipped ray of light streaming from the right side of a crucifix. This beam sprang out, withdrew, then appeared once more, drawing to it all her love. Her desires were not yet, however, fulfilled.

The following Wednesday, an ember day in Advent when the mystery of the Incarnation is especially honored in the Gospel, *Missus est Angelus Gabriel,* she received the mystical wound for which she had asked. In a later portion of her writings it is said that a friar who was preaching to the community had told them: "Love is a golden arrow, and man is in some way the master of all that he strikes with this arrow. It is then folly to attach

one's heart to earthly things and to neglect heavenly ones."
These words made such an impression on Gertrude that
she cried: "O my only Love, can I not have this arrow?
I should immediately shoot it in order to transfix and win
you forever." At once Christ offered her a golden arrow.
"You would wound me if you had a golden arrow," he
said; "but I am the one who has it. Look, I shall so wound
you that you will never recover." Thereupon he pierced
her soul with a triple-pointed arrow, leaving her more than
ever consumed by the love of God.

Among all the favors which Gertrude received, these
two—the impression of the wounds of Christ in her heart
and the piercing with the arrow of divine love—gave her
such joy, she says, that even if she were to live for a thousand years in complete desolation, she would find solace,
light, and gratitude in the remembrance of these graces.

GERTRUDE'S PROPHECIES

The saint is notable also for two prophecies. Rudolph,
emperor of the Romans, had died on July 15, 1291. In
May, 1292, as the nuns were offering prayers for the election of his successor, Gertrude informed the abbess that
Adolph of Nassau had been chosen. She added that he
would perish at the hands of one who should succeed him
—an event which occurred on July 2, 1298, when he fell
in battle with Albert of Austria. (Incidentally, the circumstances of this first prophecy prove conclusively that
the saint was not an abbess. Gertrude von Hackeborn, the
abbess, had died in 1291. The list of abbesses given by the
Solesmes editors shows that in 1292 Sophia von Mansfeld,
a descendant of the founders, was governing the community; she then was "the mother of the monastery" to
whom Gertrude told the result of the imperial election.

Every year of Gertrude's life is covered by the extant list of abbesses and interregnums; her name does not appear.)

The saint's second prophecy was made in 1294 when the community was living in dread of an impending assault by the armed forces which periodically overran the region. In this emergency the nuns decided to recite the Psalter with special antiphons in honor of the Holy Spirit. As they prayed, some members of the community recognized their shortcomings and confiding themselves to God's mercy, resolved to amend their lives. To Gertrude the effect of their contrition appeared under the image of a mist which spread through the monastery and the surrounding area, putting their enemies to flight. Just as she was assuring the abbess that the danger was averted, a messenger came to confirm her words.

ST. GERTRUDE "THE GREAT"

St. Gertrude lived and died as a simple nun. That her contemporary biographer is silent in regard to her family is probably the strongest proof that she was not of the nobility. As a rule, earlier hagiographers emphasize the worldly advantages of their subjects in order to praise the virtue of foregoing the privileges of high rank. Gertrude's companions loved her, not because of any family associations, but solely for herself. "I have exiled her from all relatives and friends," Christ said. Instead of one of the noble surnames so important in her day, St. Gertrude has the incomparable designation, "the Great," a title accorded to no other woman in Germany.

It is not because of any prominence in the external history of her country or of the Church that Gertrude has this title. As a cloistered nun she did not figure in the events of thirteenth-century Saxony. It is true that she suffered with her community from the political disorders which, as we have seen, sometimes involved the convent, but she escaped the kind of anguish suffered by her companions Sophia and Elizabeth of Mansfeld when in 1284 their own brother attacked the monastery.

St. Gertrude is "the Great" because of three things: her personality, her spiritual history, and her writings. From her own words and from the words of her contemporaries she emerges as a magnificent yet endearingly human saint, a self-effacing nun among her companions, a gracious figure marked by "the unhistorical loneliness of sanctity" to borrow Michael Harrington's happy phrase.

The Colors of Love:
The Writings of St. Gertrude

Once when St. Gertrude was wishing that she had a relic of the True Cross, Christ said to her: "Read the story of my Passion, and consider well the words that I spoke with such great love. Write them down and keep them as relics. One who wishes to recall a long-enduring affection will say to his friend, 'Remember the love you felt when you said such and such a thing to me.' He will do this rather than recall the place where they both were, the clothes they wore, or any such thing. Be sure then that the most precious relics you can have are the words in which I expressed the deepest love of my heart."

The admirers of St. Gertrude may well take these words as spoken to themselves. No relics of the saint have come down to us; the very place of her burial is unknown. Her writings are her best memorial—the intimate record of her interior life and the life of her community. Important in the history of medieval religious thought, they are valuable also as records of the customs, occupations, and human ideals of her day.

For Gertrude's preparation as a writer, her admirable abbess was chiefly responsible. Since the saint had been brought to the monastery at an early age, she must have attained her mastery of Latin there. The abbess, not yet thirty when her young namesake was entrusted to her care, had already established the strong curriculum which made Helfta famous.

St. Gertrude's literary reputation rests on her two great works, the *Exercises* and the *Legatus Divinae Pietatis* commonly known as her "Revelations."

It may also be observed here that although St. Gertrude's book is commonly called her "revelations" this designation is misleading. The original title, *Legatus Divinae Pietatis, The Messenger* (or *Herald*) *of God's Loving Kindness* is a far more accurate expression of the mission of St. Gertrude who, long before St. Margaret Mary, was to be associated with the devotion to the Sacred Heart.

The Solesmes editors, as we have observed, offer evidence to show that she was also the chief author of the *Liber Specialis Gratiae*, which records the spiritual life of St. Mechtild von Hackeborn.

A number of prayers are to be found in St. Gertrude's authentic works, but a collection of other prayers attributed to her and widely circulated is said not to be genuine.

Among the lost works of the saint are her vernacular commentaries, paraphrases and explanations of obscure passages of the Scriptures, a treatise on Esther, and a hymn in honor of the Passion. This last was evidently a cento, since she calls it "the hymn that I composed from the sayings of the saints."

Students of German literature regret the loss of these vernacular treatises. Their survival would have refuted the statement, "The vernaculars were insulated from a very real phase of life, the intellectual activity at the universities and elsewhere."

THE EXERCISES

The lesser of her two major works, the *Exercises* of St. Gertrude are spiritual reminders of the basis of Christian life, the duties and privileges of those consecrated to God, and of the necessity of preparing for the next life. The subjects of the meditations and prayers are the renewal of baptism; spiritual conversion; espousals and consecration; religious profession; acts of love of God; praise, thanksgiving, and reparation; and the coming of death.

Although a tissue of liturgical phrases and motifs, the *Exercises* nevertheless disclose Gertrude's personality in all its characteristic liberty and confidence in God. Indeed, Gertrude's timeless outlook leads her to assume the immediacy of each event in the spiritual life. Through her eyes baptism becomes a daily reality by the renewal of its promises. Similarly, the hour of death is seen as close at hand.

Of the seven spiritual exercises included in this work, the last is most noteworthy. It is this exercise which contains St. Gertrude's two allusions to the great apparition of 1281. The reference to Christ as a love-worthy youth and to her own heart as a "thorny thicket" show that she has never forgotten the manifestation of God's love which came to her in that year.

St. Gertrude employs a semi-dramatic form in this exercise and in vigorous imperatives she addresses Mercy, Peace, Truth, Wisdom, Self-oblation, Compassion, and Perseverance. Assisted by Love, the contrite sinner with whom she identifies herself reflects on the details of the life and Passion of Christ. Such personifications, common in the Middle Ages, are also found in the writings of St. Mechtild and of Mechtild von Magdeburg. A hymn found in the medieval German breviaries, and quoted in part by

Gertrude, may have suggested the personifications to all three nuns:

> Felix, quae sitit Charitas
> Te fontem vitae, Veritas.
> (Happy is Charity who thirsteth for thee
> O Truth who art the fountain of life!)[1]

Critics disagree as to the value of the *Exercises.* In *En Route,* J. K. Huysmans, speaking in the person of Durtal, finds them only an echo of the Scriptures, with none of the originality that he admires in the works of St. Teresa of Avila or of Angela of Foligno. To this the prior Maximin replies: "That is true. Gertrude does, however, resemble St. Angela by her gift of familiar conversation with Christ, and also by the loving vehemence of her assertions. But everything is transformed as it emerges—she thinks liturgically to such an extent that her least thought presents itself to her clothed in the language of the Gospels and the psalms."

Modern commentators, on the other hand, while recognizing that the *Exercises* are rooted in the liturgical forms that shaped Gertrude's spirituality, nevertheless find them original. Monsignor Gay has praised the work for its theological precision; it recalls, he says, echoing the tribute of Johannes Bühler, "both the richness of the Areopagite and the exactness of St. Thomas." The recent translation of the *Exercises* gives evidence of a new appreciation of this little spiritual classic.

THE LEGATUS

In view of the wholesale destruction of the books and manuscripts at New Helfta during the Peasants' Rebellion

[1] The Latin lines and their translation are printed in *The Exercises of St. Gertrude,* ed. a Benedictine Nun of Regina Laudis, pp. 163, 182.

of 1525, it is remarkable that any of the saint's writings survived. Yet two fifteenth-century manuscripts of the *Legatus Divinae Pietatis* are extant: one, a copy by Michael Steinbrunner in Vienna, and another in Mainz. (A manuscript at St. Gall is erroneously labeled with Gertrude's name.)

The history of the various copies and editions of the *Legatus* is involved but interesting. The first printed edition of the work, a German translation by the Dominican, Paul von Weida, was published in 1505. This version, however, is dismissed by the Solesmes editors as confused, truncated, and altered from the original. Three copies of it survive.

Issued about thirty years later, the Latin edition of the *Legatus* by the Carthusian monks Lanspergius and Loher is the best known and most important of the early publications. Unfortunately, this edition disseminated the incorrect identification of St. Gertrude with her abbess, Gertrude von Hackeborn. An ambiguous interpolation by Lanspergius led to this error although he himself did not confuse the two Gertrudes. Rather, he had a defective manuscript which lacked the first book of the *Legatus;* he supplied this deficiency by using a German redaction which he translated into Latin.

Two other Latin editions followed in 1579 and in 1599. Several more editions appeared in the sixteenth and seventeenth centuries, including Spanish, French, Italian, German, and Flemish translations of the *Legatus.* Various other writings contain excerpts from this important work.

While it is true that the *Legatus* has been published in many editions, few survive and, as the editors of the definitive Solesmes *Revelationes Gertrudianae* remark, the extant ones are not worthy of so great a saint. The work of these learned Benedictine editors has clarified the text, however, and already two French translations of their volume have appeared.

An English translation of the *Legatus* based on the edition of Dom Canteleu, O.S.B. (1602) was issued in 1870. Unfortunately, this work also perpetuates the error of confusing the saint with her abbess. To date, therefore, we do not yet have a satisfactory English translation.

St. Gertrude's book is known under three different titles. *Liber Legationis Divinae Pietatis* (or simply, *Legatus Divinae Pietatis*) is the most authentic title because it repeats a phrase occurring in chapter 3 of Book Five. *Revelations,* the title familiar to readers of the nineteenth-century English translation, has, as we have noted, a misleading connotation. Used by several editors, the title *Insinuationes Divinae Pietatis* also identifies the work. Unintentionally contributing to the confusion, the Solesmes Fathers call their two-volume edition of the works of St. Mechtild and St. Gertrude *Revelationes Gertrudianae ac Mechtildianae.* In the individual volumes, however, each work has its own proper title—*Legatus Divinae Pietatis* and *Liber Specialis Gratiae.*

Whether considered as the record of a personality, as an historical document, or as a contribution to the literature of mysticism, the five books of St. Gertrude's *Legatus* are well worth study.

Intended as a memorial tribute to the saint, the first book of this work was written after St. Gertrude's death. Book Two, the saint's masterpiece, is from her own hand and will be considered in greater detail later in the chapter. The three remaining books deal with aspects of the soul's relations with God, with the feasts of the Church, and with the deaths of members and friends of the community.

Of the five books in this work, therefore, it should be

noted that although the entire work is credited to the saint, she actually wrote only the second. Editors believe, however, that the last three books of the *Legatus* were dictated by Gertrude since they show her characteristic thought and even some of her expressions though muted and, as it were, second-hand. This delegation of authorship may be accounted for, at least in part, by St. Gertrude's frequent illnesses and also by the likelihood that she gave priority to recording the spiritual history of St. Mechtild in the *Liber Specialis Gratiae.*

Before proceeding to a more comprehensive study of Book Two, it would be well to examine the other sections of this important work in somewhat greater detail. As mentioned previously, Book One was written after Gertrude's death as a memorial tribute; it records various sayings and actions which show her holiness. The writer knew Gertrude well, and was obviously a member of the community since she says that the saint was "among us."

Of the dictated sections, Book Three, the longest, contains many chapters on the effects of holy communion. Among the other subjects treated are the love of God, the utility of prayer, and the importance of a good intention. The trials which beset the community and the more personal afflictions of illness, temptation, and discouragement find mention here also. Book Three is likewise notable as containing a passage, not hitherto remarked, which Gerard Manley Hopkins paraphrased in one of his poems. His source was obviously the English translation of 1870: "When I behold anyone in his agony who has thought of Me with pleasure, or who has performed any works deserving of reward, I appear to him at the moment of death with a countenance so full of love and mercy that he repents from his inmost heart for ever having offended **Me**, and he is saved by this repentance."

Hopkins' lines are:

> "To him who ever thought with love of me
> Or ever did for my sake some good deed
> I will appear, looking such charity
> And kind compassion at his life's last need
> That he will out of hand and heartily
> Repent he sinned and all his sins be freed."

That few readers of this poem have recognized it as a close paraphrase of St. Gertrude's lines is one of many evidences that her influence, though strong, has been, as was her cloistered life, hidden.

Book Four of the *Legatus* was, like its predecessor, compiled from the saint's dictation. It contains meditations on the feasts of the church year which were, for the most part, made when Gertrude's illnesses prevented her from attending services in the monastery church. In this section of the *Legatus,* the figures of the saints, often attired in symbolic garments, are like images from the stained glass windows of thirteenth-century cathedrals.

Book Five differs markedly from Book Four in that it is chiefly devoted to the accounts of the deaths of various persons, many of whom have already been mentioned in a previous chapter. Gertrude's own method of preparation for death is also included.

The fifth book ends with an approbation of the entire work. The "compilatrix" who had written from Gertrude's dictation asserts that the Lord held the volume to his Heart and called it "my book." When, in order to offer the work to God, this sister concealed it in her sleeve as she was about to receive holy communion, she was assured that those who read it would be guided by Christ to the passages most useful to them, as a child who is reading is guided by the finger of an older person. There is a condemnation of those who read through vain curiosity or who falsify the text. In reparation for the writer's faults of limited intelligence, lack of zeal, and inexperience, she commends the work to the Sacred Heart. The compiler feels that her defects have impaired her exposition of the secret treasures confided to her. Yet, although obliged to omit "an almost infinite number of details," she has experienced the help of the divine mercy. She concludes with the wish that readers of the book be led as by the hand, first to meditation and then to contemplation.

BOOK II: THE SPIRITUAL AUTOBIOGRAPHY

By its beauty of content and plangent cadences, Book Two stands apart from and above the other books of the *Legatus.* The most important section of this work, it contains the moving account of the conversion of St. Gertrude. Written in the first person and addressed directly to God, the book deals with the saint's mystical experiences and mirrors her exquisite and steadfast mind.

This spiritual autobiography was written with great reluctance on the part of St. Gertrude although apparently she had felt no hesitancy in writing her earlier treatises and explanations of the Scriptures. When the saint learned that it was God's will seconded by her superior's that she should write this account of her conversion and subsequent experiences, she still felt a strong repugnance. Christ answered her doubts by saying: "When St. Catherine was in prison, I visited and consoled her by the words, 'Be at peace, daughter, for I am with you.' I called John, my chosen apostle, with the words, 'Come to me, my well-beloved.' The lives of the saints show many similar occurrences. What use are they, if not to increase devotion and recall my kind tenderness toward men? By learning of these favors, others will be led to desire them for themselves, and thereby their lives will show some improvement."

Once she understood that her writing was intended to draw others to God, Gertrude's reluctance diminished somewhat. She still felt an intense surprise that Christ should treat her with such familiarity, and she knew her own community well enough to foresee that some persons would be shocked and mistrustful. Again Christ spoke, this time still more firmly: "I expect a return from my grace which has been so abundantly poured forth in you. Those who have received privileges similar to yours and have neglected them will remember, when they read your account, the graces heaped upon them and will be moved to gratitude, thereby meriting more favors. As to those perverse ones who misprize my gifts, let their sin fall on their own heads. You will lose nothing in consequence; did not the prophet say of me: 'I shall place before them a stumbling-stone?' " (A writer of our own day has observed that now it is difficult even for Catholics to believe in these graces, or "considered something shameful to admit these communications of the soul with God." Judging from Gertrude's trepidation before her own community, the attitude described was met in the thirteenth as well as in the twentieth century.)

Nevertheless, despite the Lord's assurances, Gertrude believed that she herself had not sufficiently valued God's gifts to her. Concluding the first section of this book she writes, "If you had given me as a remembrance of yourself so little a thing as a thread of flax, I ought to have received it with infinite gratitude! O God, you who know the secret of my heart, you know that it is against my inclination to write these things. Considering, however, that I have profited so little by your graces, I cannot believe that they are intended for me alone since your eternal wisdom cannot be deceived. O Giver of all good things, you who have poured out so many gifts upon me, grant that in reading this book the heart of one of your friends may be moved by your mercy and give you thanks that for the love of souls you have preserved for so long a time in my defiled heart so princely a gem. May he praise, exalt, and entreat your mercy . . . So may you be recompensed for my insufficiency."

Despite her misgivings, Gertrude began her spiritual autobiography in the spring of 1289. She was again plagued by uncertainty, however, and laid aside her work, not resuming her writing until the following October, when she was, as it were, coerced once more by the divine insistence. She records her reluctance and its overruling: "I considered it improper for me to publish these writings . . . and therefore delayed until the feast of the Exaltation of the Holy Cross. On that day, during Mass I had resolved to apply myself to another work, but the Savior triumphed over my resolution. 'Be assured,' he said, 'that you will not go out from this prison of the body before you have paid your debt to the last penny.' As I was thinking that I had already made some use of God's gifts for the benefit of my neighbor if not by writing, at least by my words, he reminded me of what I had read that very night at Matins: 'If the Lord had wished to reveal his doctrine to his contemporaries only, he would have taught by word alone and would not have inspired the sacred writers; but his teachings have been written, and today they serve for the salvation of many.' He added: 'Make no objection. I wish that your writings should be a sure and unshakable evidence of my loving kindness for the last days when I shall shower My graces on a vast number of persons.' "
(This reference to "the last days" appears to be an allusion

to the great revelation of the Sacred Heart. It occurs in St. Gertrude's well-known conversation with St. John the Evangelist and will be noted later.)

Overwhelmed by the words of Christ, Gertrude reflected on the difficulty, not to say the impossibility, of expressing in human language without scandalizing others, what she had experienced. A torrent of rain seemed to fall upon her shrinking spirit, weighing her down with more than she could absorb. She could hear only a few portentous words, the sense of which eluded her. As she appealed to God, she understood him to say: "Since this abundant rain seems to you useless, I shall draw you to my Heart, and pour out little by little what you need with gentle sweetness according to the measure of your strength." Thereafter, she found that every morning she was inspired to write a certain number of pages clearly and easily. Things of which she had known nothing before, she set down as readily as if they had been long imprinted on her memory. After completing the daily task, she found it impossible, even though she exerted all her might to write a single additional word. Yet on the following morning she could resume her work without difficulty. By this means her natural impetuosity was moderated according to the counsel: "One should not devote himself to action to such an extent that he neglects contemplation." "Thus," says Gertrude to Christ, "you permitted me sometimes to experience the joyful embraces of Rachel without depriving me of Lia's glorious fecundity. May your wise love help me to unite action and contemplation." (The association of Rachel with the contemplative and Lia with the active life is, of course, traditional.)

As she continued her writing, St. Gertrude frequently renewed her self-reproaches for having resisted the manifest will of God, and she also reiterated her motives: "You know the bottom of my heart and you know that it is for your love and glory alone that I have written these pages. May those who read them after my death be touched by the infinite kindness that compelled you to descend to the depths of my misery and to entrust such lofty gifts to one who, alas, has not esteemed them."

Having surmounted her initial reluctance to disclose the ways of God with her soul, St. Gertrude gave herself wholeheartedly to her task. With profound emotion she recalls how in her twenty-sixth year, "in a happy hour, at the beginning of twilight, thou O God of truth, more radiant than any light yet deeper than any secret thing, determined to dissolve the obscurity of my darkness. . . ." The exquisite chiaroscuro of this passage recurs throughout the book.

ST. GERTRUDE: THE WRITER

St. Gertrude's style is flexible and musical rather than marmoreal; her Latin is strongly accented, especially in exclamatory passages, and she is fond of the Virgilian formula *O ter quaterque beati.* The cadences of her Latin have caused some readers to compare her with St. Augustine. One example of a rhetorical device, typically Augustinian and incorporated in her work, is "thy wise mercy and thy merciful wisdom" *(sapienti misericordiae et misericordi sapientiae tuae).* She also utilizes grammatical modulations to emphasize successively various aspects of the Godhead—for example, *vera una Divinitas, una et trina veritas, trina et una Deitas* (from the Office of the Holy Trinity).

St. Gertrude's style, wrote one of her clerical friends with unconscious humor, "is not feminine, that is to say, not contemptible." Indeed it could on occasion be vigorous. Once when reproaching herself for failing to give

God his due, she wrote: "Alas, how many times, impelled by malice, thoughtlessness, or frivolity, have I taken back what I had given and snatched it, as it were, from between your very teeth to give to your enemy!"

LITERARY SOURCES

The saint's chief literary sources were the Scriptures, liturgical works, the writings of St. Augustine, and St. Bernard's sermons on the *Song of Songs.* We may also conclude that she knew Origen, who is mentioned in the *Liber Specialis Gratiae,* as are the writings of St. Thomas Aquinas and Albert the Great. Yet, despite her reliance on these sources, St. Gertrude always speaks with her own distinctive accent, and her style is as personal as St. Bernard's.

Many Old Testament themes and personages figure in Gertrude's writings: Noah's ark, Gideon's fleece, Joseph, Rachel, Lia, Abraham, David, Solomon. In her *Exercises* she adds Abraham, Moses, and David to the litany of the saints.[2]

Likewise, numerous scriptural and liturgical quotations are incorporated into Gertrude's text. Remembering the signs of God's love which she had received on Christmas day and reflecting with shame that she has not preserved these graces as she ought, she quotes from Isaias, XXXVIII, 14: *"Tu responde pro me, Domine Deus Meus."* (Four centuries later, Herbert's poem, "The Quip," tells how he was rebuked successively by the world, beauty, glory, money, wit, and conversation. Each stanza ends with the same Isaian refrain, "But thou shalt answer, Lord, for me.")

In addition to the more obvious scriptural and liturgical

---

[2] St. Teresa of Avila also had great devotion to David "because he too was a sinner."

expressions, such as *oriens ex alto* and *dator munerum,* Gertrude makes use of several beautiful lines from the Christmas sequence, *Laetabundus: ". . . quo sicut sidus radium protulit virgo filium verum Deum et hominem."* A favorite phrase, *creator siderum* (or sometimes *vestitor siderum*) comes from a hymn for Advent. She paraphrases the concluding lines of the *Lauda Sion* in the words, *"pascere digneris per totam huius exilii viam."*

THE IDIOM OF THE MYSTIC

The *Legatus* is a hitherto neglected source for details of life in thirteenth-century Germany. Even considered in this simple aspect, Gertrude's choice of illustrative material reveals her as a sympathetic observer, a connoisseur of human experience, to whom we may apply the eloquent words of Mme. Ancelet-Hustache, "They [the mystics] love life under all its forms."

As students of mysticism have pointed out, the language of the mystics must be properly understood; one must not insist on a literal meaning. It is necessary also to take into account the epoch, the milieu, and the intellectual and emotional character of the writer. Gertrude and the two Mechtilds all used the language of court life and chivalry as was natural for women of their temperament and environment. Evelyn Underhill has spoken of "the vividly pictorial visions of Christ and the saints which abound in the writings of the Cistercians of Helfta."[3] She sees as the source of these images not only the cycle of the liturgical year but also "the romantic vernacular poetry of the Minnesingers."

Because the language of earth is not suited to express spiritual realities, it is only by analogies and similitudes

---

[3] Evelyn Underhill, "Medieval Mysticism" in *Cambridge Medieval History* (Cambridge, 1932) VII, 796.

that these realities can be conveyed. "St. Thomas," as Walter Ong points out, "discussed the fact that metaphor, which seems to be a device distinctive of poetry and foreign to the physical and mathematical sciences and logic, turns up time and again in Christian theology." He writes: "Thus the symbolic method is common to both (poetry and theology) since neither is of itself accommodated to the human reason." *(In Sententias Petri Lombardi Commentaria, prolog,* 2.1 a 5 ad 3.) [4] Angela of Foligno declares that she cannot without some misrepresentation speak of the transcendent experiences that she has had: "Alas, the words I speak seem to me to be nothing. What am I saying? My very words cause me horror. O supreme obscurity! My words are veritable blasphemy. Silence! Silence! Silence!"

It is well-known that the Church views with great reserve the visions and revelations even of highly virtuous persons. Besides the possibility of fraud and delusions (which may be diabolical) there is also the strong possibility that if the manifestation comes from God, the visionary's account of it may be impaired by errors or exaggerations arising from preconceived ideas. "The traces of mud carried by a torrent do not originate in its source." On several occasions Gertrude did not know whether certain ideas came from God or from herself.

We are told that the personality and imagination of the visionary enter largely into his visions; Gertrude's mind and imagination were formed by God with her mission in view. Her pictures are not only dramatic and therefore instructive; they are also beautiful. If we add to this her straightforward, conversational and eloquent style, it is not hard to account for the appeal of her work.

[4] Walter J. Ong, "Wit and Mystery: A Revaluation in Mediaeval Latin Hymnody" *Speculum* XXII (1947) 324.

IMAGERY

Gertrude thought in images. It was natural for her to say to Christ: "You have overthrown the tower of my vanity and curiosity . . . you have descended to the valley of my misery." The entire *Legatus,* Book Two in particular, is filled with liturgical images: the hidden manna, the abyss of uncreated wisdom, the rose of patience.

Spiritual vestments were a recurring motif in St. Gertrude's writings. In Book Three, she had described the garments in which to receive holy communion: the innocence of Christ as a white robe; his humility as a purple tunic; his hope, as a green ornament; his love of creatures as a golden mantle; his joy in men's souls as a crown of jewels; his confidence in spite of their inconstancy, as sandals.

In Book Four, St. John the Evangelist is portrayed as wearing golden robes strewn with eagles from which a red light streams to show that he combined the highest contemplation with the remembrance of Christ's Passion. On his shoulders are golden lilies, one inscribed "The Disciple whom Jesus Loved," and the other, "This is the Guardian of the Virgin." His breastplate signifies the honor he received in reclining on the bosom of Christ at the Last Supper, and bears the first words of his gospel: *"In principio erat verbum."*

St. Benedict stands in majesty as the father of monasticism; fresh and fragrant roses spring from his body, and his sceptre is a jeweled cross. St. Mary Magdalen is adorned with golden roses and sparkling gems corresponding in number to her forgiven sins. The flowers represent the divine mercy and the jewels her acts of penance. St. Bernard's robe is tri-colored: white for innocence, violet for fidelity to monastic life, crimson for fervent love. He wears golden bracelets set with gems in honor of his excellent doctrine and preaching. A diadem of many colors crowns his heart to show the profit that others have gained from his writings. As St. Gertrude thanks God for the graces given to St. Bernard, small gold shields engraved with the names of various virtues appear on his garments.

The vestments of St. Augustine glow like pure crystal with the colors of purity, humility, and charity. Above his head a radiant globe sends forth rays and stars in honor of the dedication of his mind to God. St. Catherine of Alexandria, seated in royal state, is surrounded by the fifty philosophers whom she converted, each holding a golden sceptre with which he touches the hem of her robe. St. John the Baptist wears vestments of crimson ornamented with golden lambs. St. Dominic and St. Francis, like St. Benedict are brilliant with flowers and jeweled sceptres.

On the day of the Assumption, our Lady appeared, clothed in a green mantle shining with many golden flowers in the form of a trefoil. To prepare for this feast, Gertrude had intended to offer as many Hail Marys as the Blessed Virgin had spent years on earth (the number is conjectured by various persons as sixty-three, sixty-six, or seventy) but because of her extreme weakness, she had been able to say only the three aspirations, *"Ave Maria, gratia plena, Dominus tecum."* The trefoils on Mary's garments represented this threefold ejaculation.

The robes of Christ, as she visualized him on Ascension Day, were a green tunic symbolizing the living freshness of the virtues of his holy humanity, and a scarlet mantle symbolizing the love that led him to his Passion.

On the first Sunday of Lent, as Gertrude prayed that Christ might supply for the dispensation from the fast which she was obliged to accept, she was consoled by seeing herself in garments representing all the virtues that she desired: a white robe for the innocence which the privations of Christ had won for her, and a red robe for the merits of his abstinence. A number of ornaments signified the many bodily labors which the work of our salvation had cost the Son of God.

On the feast of All Saints, a golden amice clothed her as she shared in the merits of the blessed; and on Gaudete Sunday, a purple garment. Others for whom she prayed she saw in robes which symbolized the virtues of innocence, humility, and charity—a white tunic, precious stones in the form of violets, and a rose-colored mantle covered with golden flowers.

Similarly vivid descriptions appear in the writings of St. Mechtild von Hackeborn, as we have already noted. The popular and religious literature of the Middle Ages offers other examples—one is "The Garment of Good Ladies" by Robert Henryson, the Scottish Chaucerian.

References to spiritual armor in the *Legatus* no doubt derive ultimately from St. Paul's admonition to put on the armor of God *(Ephesians,* VI, 13-17 and *I Thess.* V, 8).

THE TREE OF LOVE

It is in the second book that the colorful and enchanting image of the tree of love occurs. Gertrude was attending mass, and overcome by weariness, was roused by the bell at the elevation. It seemed to her that she saw the Lord Jesus holding a tree covered with marvelous fruits and leaves which shone like stars and sent forth brilliant rays. He distributed the fruits to the saints, and then planted the tree in Gertrude's heart as in a garden that she might be sustained by its fruits and refreshed by its shade. Instantly she began to pray for a person who had caused her to suffer, and at the same time she saw a lovely flower appear on the tree. If she persevered in her good will, she realized, this blossom would produce the fruit of charity.

On the same day, Christ reappeared to her under the form of a comely young man. He asked her to gather nuts from the tree to offer to him, and lifted her into the branches that she might do so. With her usual courteous forthrightness, the saint pointed out that it would be more fitting for him to gather the nuts for her—after all, she was a woman and not strong. Christ gave her to understand that it is for us to obey him exactly and fully, even to the point of "breaking our own will." She hastened thereupon to gather the nuts for him, and as she did so, he seated himself beside her and asked her to remove the shells. Gradually she realized the allegorical significance of the tree: the nuts growing among delicious fruits represent those persons of hard and bitter disposition to whom, as well as to the gentle, we owe charity.

On another occasion she saw the tree of charity growing from the Sacred Heart. It was tall and very fair, filled with both flowers and fruits among leaves as brilliant as the stars. Both the fruits and the flowers sent out an exquisite perfume. From the roots arose a pure fountain which mounted to a great height and then returned to its source. This image represented the marvelous union of the humanity and the divinity in Christ, the mystery which brings spiritual joy and refreshment to the human race.

Her own transformation in Christ was represented by a series of images, beginning with a little plant growing near the burning Heart of Jesus under the influence of his divine love. Yet blighted by her faults and negligences, the plant shrank away until it resembled a cinder. As she invoked the mercy of Christ, the streams of blood and water from the Sacred Heart revived the lifeless coal, which then assumed the form of a flowering tree, its branches divided into three parts "like a lily." Christ presented the tree to the Holy Trinity, and each of the three divine persons attached to one of the branches all the fruits that Gertrude would have produced had she corresponded perfectly to the inspirations of God's omnipotence, wisdom, and love.

After communion, she saw her soul again under the form of a tree rooted in the wound of Christ's side; a marvelous sap arose in it causing fruits to appear through the strength of his divinity and humanity. The Trinity rejoiced in this tree as did also the company of the saints, who hung upon its branches golden crowns representing their merits. In a wonderful manifestation of the communion of saints, Gertrude saw that the fruits of the tree began to distill a precious liquor, of which one part rose to heaven augmenting the joys of the blessed, another part flowed into purgatory assuaging the sufferings of the souls there, and the third part spread over the earth bringing consolation to the good and the healthful bitterness of penance to sinners. This phenomenon occurred in answer to Gertrude's prayer that since her negligence had deprived others of benefits, these others might have some share in God's mercy to her.

The life of a religious for whom the saint was praying also appeared under the form of a magnificent tree with leaves as brilliant as gold, growing before the throne of the Most High. This person climbed into the tree and began to cut off certain branches which had begun to wither. As she removed each one, another grew from the throne of God, and being grafted on the tree, immediately brought forth beautiful crimson fruit which she presented to Christ. The branches coming forth from the throne of God and replacing the withered ones represented the holy life of Christ, whose sufferings and merits compensated for her

106

faults; the fruits represented her good will in correcting her defects.

Even before its occurrence in the twelfth-century treatise, *De Fructibus Carnis et Spiritus* by Hugh of St. Victor, the image of the tree of virtues and the tree of vices was a commonplace in the Middle Ages. It was also used in miniatures.

The tree of charity in *Piers Plowman* is probably the example most familiar to English readers: In answer to the question, "What is the meaning of charity?" Anima replies:

> Then to tell you truly, it is a fair tree . . .
> Mercy is the main root of it, and the mid-stock is pity,
> The leaves are loyal words and the law of Holy Church,
> The blossoms are obedient speech and a benign bearing . . .
> And so through God and through good men groweth the
>   fruit, charity . . . "
> "It grows," said he, "in a garden of God's making,
> The shoot is from that stock and shelters in man's body,
> And the heart is the home wherein it rises."
>   (H. G. Wells' version)

Finally, on the feast of Pentecost, as St. Gertrude prayed for the gifts of the Holy Spirit, she saw these gifts as trees differing in their fruits—for example, fear of the Lord was shown by little spikes from which flowers grew; the trees of knowledge and piety distilled dew gently; counsel and fortitude were symbolized by golden cords on the tree; wisdom and understanding by streams of nectar.

THE LANCE

Another image of special interest in the writings of the saint is that of the lance. As Gertrude's name is variously interpreted "spear maiden," "dear lance," and "spear strength," there would seem to be a particular significance attached to such a passage as "The eye of my beloved which pierces my heart is the confidence which she ought to have in me." When she was trying to chant the office with all possible fervor in honor of God and the saint whose feast was being celebrated, she saw the words "darting like lances from her heart to the Heart of Jesus and causing him inexpressible delight. From the point of the lances streamed rays of light like stars which glorified all the saints, but especially the one whose feast was being celebrated." It will be recalled that the piercing of Gertrude's heart by the arrow of divine love had been preceded by her desire to pierce the Heart of Christ by the golden arrow of her love.

When Gertrude saw the protecting angels guarding the convent, she desired to know how all might share in this safe-keeping. Christ said to her, "Let them make shields for themselves—small below by humility, and broad above by confidence in my goodness." (Mechtild von Magdeburg also prescribes spiritual armor: "your sword, the noble rose, Jesus Christ; your buckler, the white lily, Mary.")

Flower images are likewise to be found in the *Legatus.* St. Gertrude's prayer to our Lady begins, "Hail, O white lily of the glorious and ever-peaceful Trinity! Hail, Rose of heavenly beauty! Of you the King of Heaven wished to be born; by your milk he was nourished; nourish our souls with divine influence." (Huysmans in *En Route* praises this prayer.)

The saint's writing is notable also for her use of synesthesia—the fusing of sense impressions in a manner that anticipates Shelley, the French imagists, and Edith Sitwell, to name only a few later writers. She speaks of jewels and flowers emitting melody; the golden wings of the angels are also musical. Precious stones representing humility have not only the form but the odor of violets.

The foregoing examples demonstrate that to express the sweetness of the divine union, Gertrude draws on all the senses for images, as St. Bernard had done before her. Yet she is always profoundly peaceful; *serene* is one of her favorite words. (In this respect her writing contrasts with the frequent restlessness and self-consciousness of Mechtild von Magdeburg's.)

SIMILITUDE

Another important aspect of the saint's writings is her extensive use of the so-called "similitude."

In the *Legatus,* St. Gertrude frequently employs these comparisons or analogies to illustrate spiritual truths. Such similitudes enable her to write clearly about even the most exalted experiences. Three centuries later, in St. Teresa's images of the watering of the spiritual garden and of the spiritual mansions, we find the same device. Both Gertrude and Teresa acknowledge the limitations of these figures of speech; Gertrude does so by introducing them with the words, *ad similitudinem,* or less often, *verbi gratia.* In the *Legatus* they range from comparisons drawn from nature, through chivalric and feudal details, to simple domestic situations. They are quite distinct from the imaginative visions of the saint. Gertrude's similitudes are historically valuable as vignettes showing many aspects of thirteenth-century life.

In the similitudes drawn from nature, the sun as the image of God is of course a classic comparison. From Dante to Edith Sitwell it has been used by religious poets. Images of fire and water, rain and dew are also familiar in mystical writing—both St. Gertrude and Teresa of Avila are particularly fond of water. (Speaking of the Spanish mystic, Walsh has said: "Mountains and prairies, birds and flowers, clouds and sunshine, and above all, water—

beautiful, sparkling, elusive water—everything she saw was like the pages of a book in which she could read how wonderful and how good was God."[5])

In Gertrude's writings, the soul drawn by God is absorbed as a dewdrop is taken up by the noon-day sun; the rain of grace falls with such abundance that she is weighed down like a delicate young plant. Fields, orchards, and gardens, familiar sights to the community at Helfta, figure occasionally in the similitudes. References to flowers are usually general, only lilies, roses, and violets being specified.

Comparisons with animals are more lively and original. When the community chanted *"Regnum mundi et omnem ornatum saeculi contempsi,"* the demons "fled as quickly as a pack of rabid dogs when someone has thrown hot water on them." (Mechtild von Magdeburg in her *Lux Fluens* usually refers to dogs as contemptible, useless, or dangerous.) Wolves, foxes, oxen, lambs, doves, the pelican, fish, and bees also provide comparisons. A detail of medieval life emerges from the comment, "If a wife sometimes gives food to her husband's falcons, she will not for that reason be deprived of his embraces."

THE IMAGE OF LOVE

Parents and children also figure in many of St. Gertrude's similitudes. (In this respect, her examples differ from those of her friend, St. Mechtild, who rarely mentions children.) Remembering that Gertrude was only five when she was brought to Helfta, one asks where she learned the intimate details of family life. She was, of course, intelligent beyond her years and she may have remembered scenes of home. Probably she also listened

[5] William T. Walsh, *Saint Teresa of Avila* (Milwaukee, 1943) p. 53.

intently to the reminiscences of her companions. The affectionate reunions of parents with children at the convent school must likewise have given her some vicarious experience. Then too, her own womanly heart would have an instinctive knowledge of parental love.

Once when Christ asked her if she had ever seen a mother console a little child, she was silent because she could not remember. Then he brought to her mind the recollection of such a scene six months earlier. The child must have been very young, for only the mother could understand what it was saying. By this image Gertrude was impressed with the realization that God alone fully understands the minds of his creatures. "The mind of another is a dark forest."

Other similitudes involving the relations of parents and children are vivid and charming. A mother who is working with silk or pearls will put her little child in an elevated place so that he may hold her thread and jewels. A father is glad to see himself surrounded by his many children who arouse the admiration of others. "But seeing among these children the smallest one, who is less attractive than the others, this good father, filled with pity, takes it into his arms and gives it many little presents." Gertrude considered herself to be like this little child, less worthy of admiration than her sisters, but for that very reason, favored by God's compassion. She speaks also of a practice followed by a mother who wishes to keep a beloved little son with her. When he desires to run out to play with his companions, she will place masks *(larvas)* or some other terrifying objects near by, in order that the frightened child may run back to her arms.

Once when Gertrude saw two members of the community disputing, one upholding justice and the other charity, she appealed to Christ who said: "A father who

111

sees his children contending in play will not interfere unless there is danger of a real quarrel." In another similitude she observes that a mother would gladly deck her small child with gold and silver, but since he cannot bear their weight, she adorns him with flowers instead.

Other passages refer to the father presiding at table and enjoying the skill of an entertainer who is performing for his guests; seeing that the cellar is well stocked with wine; correcting a son, or teaching a daughter. Mothers are depicted guiding a girl's hand at work, giving medicine to a sick child, or selecting ornaments for a girl's holiday attire. On the whole, this group of similitudes gives an attractive picture of family life.

Many of St. Gertrude's comparisons refer to husbands and wives, especially at the time of marriage. Both bride and bridegroom are assumed to be of noble, or even of royal rank. Similitudes of this kind show not only a richly ceremonious setting, but also a loving confidence between husband and wife. Several comparisons treat of the preparations for marriage: for example, when a lord is about to celebrate his wedding, he stores up quantities of grain and wine at harvest time, and immediately the rumor flies that he is intending to marry. Likewise, when a girl sees many messengers coming from her bridegroom to negotiate the marriage, she also must make some preparations. However eager as she may be to hasten to her husband, nevertheless a bride will take time to adorn herself and to make gifts for him.

A king about to marry a bride who lives far away will send a great company of nobles to escort her with musical instruments and many presents. When she arrives, he will establish her honorably in one of his royal palaces, and in the presence of all his princes, he will give her the ring of betrothal. The bride, however, prefers the caresses of her husband to the applause of the populace. In her own home, among her own people, she may act more freely than can her bridegroom when he comes to visit her. If on these occasions she appreciates his reserve and treats him graciously, he will not fail to receive her into his home with corresponding affection when the time comes. The spiritual realities underlying these similitudes are obvious.

The affection of friends also supplies many comparisons. The exchange of gifts and confidences, taking meals together, and consoling each other are frequently mentioned. Gertrude emphasizes the generosity of friends—a rich man will offer his money-box; he will clothe his friend in fine garments. A true friend will rise with alacrity even from a deep sleep for the sake of conversing with his friend. When Gertrude adds that such love is the more appreciated if he be one who ordinarily cannot sleep, her remark gains force from the fact that she herself suffered from insomnia.

THE PANORAMA OF MEDIEVAL LIFE

The many families who had contact with Helfta either through blood-relationship or through benefactions doubtless afforded ample information concerning feudal manners and the customs of court life. The king or emperor and his attendants supplied analogues for members of the heavenly court. Gertrude's similitudes rarely show the sovereign alone, but rather in actions such as releasing prisoners, visiting his queen, clothing and feeding a faithful knight, giving and accepting presents, providing for the widow and children of a devoted follower, and receiving captives.

In a similitude intended to emphasize that a person whom God has honored should have manners conformable to his dignity, she declares that it would be shameful for one who has been asked to serve at the king's table to go out to clean the horse-stalls and thereby defile himself. Similarly, a chamberlain who has been given the honor of supporting an aged or infirm king at the table would behave reprehensibly, if rising hastily to serve, he allowed his master to fall. All three of the nun-writers at Helfta, Gertrude and the two Mechtilds employ such feudal comparisons; the two latter put special emphasis on the long and arduous training required for those who would serve at court.

Gertrude's similitudes also show some familiarity with professions, arts, and crafts. As might be expected, many scenes from the schoolroom appear in her writings. She remarks that a kind teacher takes a young pupil into his arms to point out the letters, correct mistakes, and supply omissions. She observes that students must begin with the alphabet before advancing to logic. In another similitude she mentions the use of crystal to magnify script. The activities of the physician, of the goldsmith, and of the painter also supply her with illustrations. Cloistered though she is, she is acquainted with the hunter's attitude and observes that he takes greater pleasure in the flesh of a wild beast caught after long pursuit than he does in that of domestic animals.

Gold and jewels figure in some similitudes. More than once St. Gertrude remarks that gold appears to best advantage when it is contrasted with black or with colors. A noble maiden who knows how to make artistic ornaments of pearls and other gems to adorn herself and her sister brings honor to her father, her mother, and all the household. Gold and silver may be melted together, she says, to form a precious amalgam—this is a figure of the union of the divinity and humanity. Imitation jewelry made of copper and glass can give an appearance of wealth; but persons who wear real gold and gems are accounted richer. A passage of great interest refers to a precious stone, called a besant, worn in the emperor's crown "by reason of its singularity." (Editors have been puzzled by this word, which ordinarily denotes a coin.)

Some effective comparisons are based on the use of perfumes and sweet spices. Delicate ladies, says the saint, prefer perfume to any other gift. When a jar of spices is stirred, it sends forth fragrance; whether the stirring is done with a wooden stick or with something more valuable does not matter. So unworthy persons can provide opportunity for the exercise of virtue.

The saint's frank humility as well as humor appears when she compares herself to a scarecrow *(tamquam larvam)* in an orchard to protect the fruit from birds. Evidently the fruits are her sisters; the birds are evil spirits.

ANALOGY

These and other spiritual realities, Gertrude realized, can be described only by analogy. In various ways throughout her writings, therefore, she warns her readers that her language is not to be taken literally: *"ut humano more loquar,"* she will say. Again, in her account of a special grace which she received at Christmas, Gertrude writes: "As I possessed it (the Divine Infant) within me, it seemed to me that all at once I was changed into the color of this Divine Infant, if we may be permitted to call that color which cannot be compared to anything visible."

A passage from St. Bernard is of great value in supplementing Gertrude's explanation and clarifying the nature of such images: ". . . When something from God *(divinitus)* has momentarily and, as it were, with the swiftness of a flash of light shed its ray upon the mind in ecstasy of spirit, whether for the tempering of this too great radiance, or for the sake of imparting it to others, forthwith there present themselves, whence I know not, certain imaginary likenesses of lower things, suited to the meanings which have been infused from above, by means of which that most pure and brilliant ray of truth is in a manner shaded, and becomes both more bearable to the soul itself and more capable of being communicated . . . I think that these images are formed in us by the suggestions of the holy angels. . . ." *(Cant.* XLI, 3. Dom John Chapman's translation.)

In the introduction to their edition of the *Legatus,* the Solesmes Benedictines say that Gertrude's first visions were imaginative. As her union with Christ developed, his communications were not through images, but *"per puriores illuminationes cognitionum,"* and at the end of her life were of such a nature that she could hardly express them.

A passage in Book Four of the *Legatus* indicates that when Gertrude wondered why the Lord so often instructed her by means of corporeal visions, she was told that just as in former times the incarnation, passion, and resurrection were prefigured to the prophets by means of mystical figures and similitudes, so now also spiritual and invisible realities which transcend the human understanding must be likewise shown by similitudes or analogies. "No one therefore should scorn what is manifested under a corporal likeness but rather endeavor to become worthy of tasting the hidden sweetness."

The modern historian of mysticism, Juan Arintero, speaks in a similar vein: "Although they (the saints) see that these things are incomprehensible, they are nevertheless able to declare these marvels by means of analogies, especially when God himself suggests certain symbols which are more suitable for representing them."[6]

Some of the dialogues between Christ and the soul, as Vernet notes, are not to be taken as actual, literal conversations. The expression, "Jesus said to me," which one finds in many writings besides St. Gertrude's "refers to the thoughts which occur during prayer."[7]

The limitations of ordinary language have thwarted many saints. Sigrid Undset writes of St. Catherine of Siena: "She who had the whole of the lovely and rich Tuscan language at her disposal said: 'It is impossible; it is like dipping pearls into mud.' " Arintero expresses the same idea: "The visions and locutions of the spiritual senses, although they offer a certain analogy with the bodily senses, which authorizes the use of the same names, transcend every form and figure."[8]

In a treatise, "Studies on the Phenomena of Mystical Experience," A. Léonard, O.P., points out that mystical experience is linked to objective realities: Scripture, the Church, the sacraments. It "can not discover new truths; it is detached neither from revelation nor from faith. . . . The mystic can attach no weight to his intuition except in so far as it reveals to him more intensely what he already knows in common with all Christians."[9] The solidity of St. Gertrude's doctrine, the simplicity of her counsels, and the directness of her expression put her into the main-

---

[6] Juan Arintero, *The Mystical Evolution in the Development and Vitality of the Church,* trans. Jordan Aumann, O.P. (St. Louis, 1949) II, 355.

[7] Felix Vernet, *La Spiritualité Médiévale* (Paris, 1928) p. 195.

[8] Arintero, II, 340.

[9] A. Léonard, O.P. "Studies in the Phenomenon of Mystcal Experience" in *Mystery and Mysticism: A Symposium* (New York, 1956) pp. 92-93.

stream of spirituality. Ardor and serenity are equally characteristic of "this royal soul" as Vernet calls her.

St. Gertrude's vocation was to teach, not only her own sisters, but whomever should read her writings. Today we realize the effectiveness of the picture as a teaching device. In the last chapter of Book Two, the saint explains the necessity for her pictorial style when she expresses the hope that her readers may be led "through these descriptions and images to taste for themselves the hidden manna which can be known only by means of figures."

The approbation of St. Gertrude's writings came first of all from those who had known the saint. Foremost among these is Theodore of Apoldia, a Dominican, whom the Master General commissioned to write the life of St. Dominic. Theodore had not only examined the writings of St. Gertrude, but he had had many conversations with her. The superiors of the monastery at Helfta also secured the approval of other theologians, both Dominican and Franciscan, six of whom are named in the Vienna codex.

Except for the two fifteenth-century manuscripts mentioned earlier in this chapter, there is little evidence of St. Gertrude's fame during the two centuries after her death; it is possible, however, that an underground influence may yet come to light. The history of German spirituality during the fourteenth century is not complete. One hint of the saint's reputation is found in a fourteenth-century manuscript of the *Liber Specialis Gratiae* at Eisleben. In this, the saint's writing is referred to as that of *"sanctissimae virginis Trute."*[10]

Johannes Bühler has said: "It may well be that the outpourings of love of a St. Hildegard, Gertrude of Helfta, or Mechtild of Hackeborn are not as immediate in their

[10] Trutha, Truda, Drudis, and Druda are other diminutive forms of her name occasionally found.

appeal to modern sensibilities as the speculations of a Meister Eckhart are, or the tender expressions of a Suso. Still their disposition of heart and soul is no less deep and their language—unfortunately Latin—is often just as poetic."[11]

St. Gertrude's final prayer for the readers of her *Legatus* gives expression both to her largeness of heart and to the "serene humility" for which her companions loved her: "According to your faithful promise and the lowly desire of my heart, grant to all who humbly read these writings to rejoice in your condescension, to pity my unworthiness, and with compunction to desire their own perfection, so that from the golden censers of their hearts burning with love a sweet fragrance may rise to you, atoning fully for all my faults of negligence and ingratitude."

[11] J. Bühler, *Klosterleben in Deutschen Mittelalter nach Zeitgenossischen Aufzeichnungen* (Leipzig, 1923), p. 248.

Gertrude in Her Community

St. Gertrude was a full-time member of her community. Many of her special graces came to her as she took part in the ordinary routine of convent life. It was just after she had bowed to an elderly sister, "according to our rule," that she was called by God to a new life of union with him. Eight years later she was with the community awaiting the signal to go to the infirmary where communion was to be given to a sister, when she was inspired by the Holy Spirit to write the account of this great apparition.

When, with the other sisters, she received her portion of food and clothing, Gertrude simply took whatever came first to hand without showing any fastidiousness. She did, however, value her tools in God's service: her book, her stylus, her writing tablet. When she received presents, she gave them away either to the poor or "to persons hostile to her." Her biographer declares that when she gave something to her neighbor it was with the alacrity of a miser who receives a hundred coins for one.

Whatever was necessary for her physical life—sleep, food, clothing—she used as for God living within her; in the same spirit she went from one activity to the next, desiring in all to be another humanity for Christ.

120

Although her role as teacher distinguished her from some of the other members of the community, Gertrude sought to efface herself in her spiritual exercises. When the revelation of God's love moved her to tears, she tried to conceal them. When she was inspired to perform certain ceremonies in honor of the Passion and to pray with her arms extended, she remarked, "One who practices such a prayer ought to hide himself in some remote place, for it is not the custom to pray thus." (Since her time, the custom has become less uncommon, as the Solesmes editors observe.)

Gertrude showed special affection for the sisters who had arduous or uncongenial duties. In one passage she speaks of a sister who received a great reward from God because she did not complain when she had to work beyond her strength. For a person whose duties in the kitchen prevented her from praying as she wished, the saint was given this message from Christ: "I did not choose her to serve me for only an hour daily, but to live with me all day long without interruption. She will do this if she performs all her actions for my glory with the same fervor as she prays. She should also desire that those who profit by her labor should not only be fortified in body but should likewise be confirmed in good and make progress in my love. If she does this, her actions will be to me like delicious food carefully prepared."

Similarly, when an accident to one of the sisters might have necessitated an amputation, Gertrude prayed fervently that this calamity might be averted. Christ reassured her, adding that the sufferer would be richly recompensed for her patience and that all who helped to relieve her pain would share in her reward.

To another of her companions, a sister who had wondered why God required her to endure a trial beyond her strength, St. Gertrude brought this message from Christ: "Ask her what trial would be proportioned to her strength, and tell her that since the kingdom of heaven cannot be won without suffering, she shall choose now the sufferings that suit her; then when they come, let her bear them patiently."

In consoling her sisters Gertrude derived confidence from Christ's assurance that he never permits his own to be tried beyond their strength, but moderates their adversity, "even as a mother who wishes to warm her little child at the fire always holds her hand between the fire and her child."

It was Gertrude's conviction that God's gifts bore no fruit in her unless she shared them by her words and her writings. The magnificence of these gifts did not lighten the labor of sharing them, and she was often extremely weary. From early in the morning until evening she was studying, teaching, and writing. Christ had said to her: "I am always hungry and thirsty for the salvation of souls; anyone who will study some words of Scripture every day will appease my hunger."

Gertrude worked quickly and with such apparent pleasure that she seemed rather to be enjoying herself than laboring. St. Mechtild saw her friend always facing the throne of God as she passed from one activity to another. Yet the long hours of study, reading, writing, and teaching often brought her to the point of exhaustion—"my inertia" she calls it. Once when she performed a difficult task, saying, "Lord, I offer this action to thee through thy only Son, in the strength of thy holy Spirit, and for thy eternal glory," she was made to understand that this dedication gave her work an extraordinary value. Needless to say, she expected neither thanks nor praise from those for whom she worked, although even persons who failed to appreciate her holiness could not help admiring her intelligence and eloquence.

TEACHER AND COUNSELOR

In her special duty of teaching the Scriptures Gertrude was tireless. She would paraphrase difficult passages so that unlearned sisters could better understand them. When discussing texts which recount gross actions, she was so impersonal that only a slight flush betrayed her embarrassment. If it was necessary to treat such matters in order to help someone in spiritual difficulty, she spoke with complete candor and tranquility. In all her studies God was her teacher—*Tu optime magistrorum,* she calls him: "O best of teachers, you who have so many times instructed my stupidity."

It was not only by curing the "wound of ignorance" that Gertrude served her sisters. Convinced that the marks of God's love were given to her for the benefit of others, she often asked: "How may my sisters share this grace, O Lord?" She sincerely considered every member of the community to be better than herself. Others, she thought, by the greater purity and holiness of their lives gave more glory to God by a single thought than she could by the holocaust of her whole life, unworthy and negligent as she was. (One is reminded of St. Teresa's remark: "The best sign of improvement is not raptures, ecstasy, sweetness in prayer . . . but thinking oneself the most wicked of all.")

A lesson which St. Gertrude longed to impress on her sisters was the importance of fervor and recollection at work and prayer. Characteristically, she taught this by means of three graphic comparisons: works done through custom and routine, she said, were recorded in black ink; those done in memory of the Passion were recorded in red; those done solely for the honor of God, to obtain the salvation of all through the merits of Christ's sufferings, with complete renunciation of all personal merit were recorded in gold. Gradations of fervor were also represented by pearls symbolizing the words of the penitential psalms recited at the chapter of faults. Words spoken through habit and without ardor appeared under the form of dark, lustreless pearls, while those recited devoutly were brilliant. The most striking of all these images is associated with the feast of the Nativity of our Lady, when St. Gertrude saw each sister's guardian angel standing beside her with a branch in his hand. Various kinds of flowers and fruits, representing the devotion of each nun, sprang from the branches; at the end of the office the angels brought them to adorn the throne of the Blessed Virgin.

Her admonition gained force from her realization that her own recitation of the office was sometimes imperfect. When on one occasion she showed less than her usual exactness, she was startled to discover a demon beside her derisively repeating the words, *"mirabilia testimonia tua"* and mocking her careless pronunciation. "Yes!" he exclaimed at the end of the psalm, "truly your Creator, your Savior, the friend of your soul has done well to give you such facility in speech! You have a great talent for eloquent discourse on any subject whatsoever, but when you speak to God your words come forth at such a rate that in a single psalm you have left out so many letters, syllables, and words!" On hearing this, Gertrude reflected that those who habitually recite the office negligently might have to answer for this fault at the hour of death.

It was as the servant of her sisters that Gertrude taught them, advised, consoled, and prayed for them. She had the gift of dispelling doubts and correcting false ideas. Yet though so enlightened in counseling others, she was also quick to seek advice, even consulting persons who might have been considered inferior to herself, and humbly following their recommendations.

Her advice to those who consulted her must have been succinct as well as apt, for we are told that she spoke to many in a single hour. Yet though brief, her words were so effective that sometimes her hearers were moved to tears. Among those whom she directed were "a learned person," "an ignorant person," "one who had entered religion at an advanced age" (perhaps this was Mechtild von Magdeburg), a person tried by temptation, an invalid, and one who found great difficulty in the work she had been assigned. The subjects of Gertrude's instructions to those who came to her were, as might be expected, confidence in God's love and mercy, and the means of pleasing him. "Many things please me," Christ had told her. The apparition of St. Mary Magdalen whose ornaments of flowers and jewels corresponded in number to her forgiven sins was only one of the many images whereby Gertrude was impressed by God's willingness to accept the penitent.

Once as St. Mechtild was praying for her friend, she saw Gertrude's heart under the image of a firm bridge walled on one side by the divinity, on the other by the humanity of Christ. He said to her, "Those who come to me by this bridge will not fall nor wander from the right way."

To share God's gifts by her words through teaching and advising was, Gertrude understood, to make good use of her "talent of understanding." Yet occasionally she accused herself of wasting in useless words the eloquence with which Christ had blessed her. Moreover, those who came to her for counsel sometimes applied to her the words of Ecclesiastes: "Sharp goads they are to sting us, sharp nails driven deep home, these wise words!" Yet she herself was cut to the heart if someone with the intention of consoling her, advised her to leave incorrigible persons to bear the ultimate penalty of their misdeeds. Her answer was that she would rather die. Such was her burning sincerity that to her contemporary biographer, her words seemed to be "dyed in her heart's blood." For Gertrude, the agonizing question was, how could God be appeased? She saw her own faults no less clearly than her neighbor's. One is reminded of St. Bridget of Sweden, who on being asked by our Lady, "What are the proud ladies of Sweden talking about?" answered, "I am one of them, and I am ashamed to tell you."

WIDE APOSTOLATE

Other classes of persons, from the laborers on the convent property to the Dominican fathers and brothers from Halle and Magdeburg, also engaged Gertrude's interest and compassion. (Yet it is recorded that she never looked at any man long enough to recognize him on a second meeting.) The affection that she inspired drew her friends to God, and "even rebels" says her biographer, who would not humble themselves before anyone else, were overcome by her. Some persons declared that her words touched them more deeply than the long sermons of better preachers. To her as to Jeremias the Lord had said: "I have put my words into your mouth."

Gertrude's gift of dispelling doubts and restoring peace of soul might well make her the special patron of counselors. Even the abbess consulted her. Sometimes the saint was unaware of what she had done for others: a sister who was tormented by temptations which made her hesitate to receive holy communion was at once delivered from her trouble when she secretly possessed herself of a scrap of worn-out cloth from Gertrude's garments.

Gertrude's charity was not limited to the members of her community. Like Christ she "had compassion on the multitude." She prayed for Jews and pagans, and was deeply concerned for their salvation. She prayed for all sinners, for the souls in Purgatory, for the afflicted, for prelates, and for her superiors. Many persons whom she did not know were recommended to her, and she faithfully interceded for them, sending them sympathetic messages as well. She obtained copies of the Scriptures for places that lacked them. Even animals shared her compassion, especially when she saw them undergoing cold, hunger, or thirst. She would offer to God as a tribute of praise the suffering of his irrational creatures, imploring him to have pity on the works of his hands and deliver them from their pain.

The scope of Gertrude's charity is expressed in her cry: "O my Savior, I wish to bring to you every soul that you might take delight in each. I would go from now till doomsday to carry to you everyone who does not know you and whose love could please you!"

The magnanimity shown in her prayers for many classes of people was accompanied by sound practical sense and realization of the fact that some are called to one state of life, some to another. These qualities no doubt attracted her many visitors. A quotation which she uses in the third of her *Exercises* illustrates her understanding of human nature and its aspirations: "How could our soul, being encased in mortal flesh, overcome the law of nature, licentious liberty, the force of custom, and the urge of youth, if thou didst not, through our free will, kindle within us this love of chastity, nourish this desire in our hearts, and give us the strength to accomplish it? . . . For while no prohibition lesseneth the honor of marriage, and the initial blessing ever remaineth upon holy matrimony, nonetheless some loftier souls are found who, turning aside from the conjugal union of man and wife, desire the mystery which lieth hid therein; and, without seeking to imitate that which is wrought in marriage, love what is signified thereby." (From the Preface for the Consecration of Virgins.)

The rubric in the second *Exercise* also shows her awareness of those outside the cloister: "Beseech the Virgin Mother that she may be thy guide in the monastic state or in whatever thy state of life may be."

It seems abundantly clear that as a rule Gertrude did not give unsought advice, but that her admonitions were only to those who came to her for help. Of St. Bernard it was remarked, "His charity appears even in his reproaches and shows that he reproves to correct, never to insult." The same might be said of St. Gertrude. Some persons in distress of mind were advised in dreams to have recourse to her. The contemporary biographer who reports this observes that although the relief of mental pain is not so obvious as the cure of bodily disease, it may sometimes be as truly miraculous.

St. Mechtild once protested to Christ that Gertrude judged the faults of others with some severity. She received the reply that as the saint could not tolerate the least stain on her own soul, so she could not endure with indifference the faults of her neighbor. Gertrude herself sometimes wondered whether she should correct others, although her motive was always the consuming desire that God should have all the honor due him, especially from those who had vowed to serve him. Once when she was reading to the community, she pronounced with such emphasis the words of the great commandment, "Thou shalt love the Lord thy God with thy whole heart, with thy whole soul, with thy whole mind, and with all thy strength," that her contemporary biographer cites the incident as evidence of her zeal for God's glory. (According to one account, she read the text twice, perhaps unconsciously.)

Once in a vision, Gertrude saw Christ supporting a great mansion which seemed ready to fall. "Look," he told her, "see how much labor I undergo to hold up this dear house of religion. It is everywhere threatened with ruin because so few will work faithfully or suffer anything to defend and sustain it. . . . All those who by word or act maintain the religious state are like so many columns to hold it up." Profoundly touched by this sight, Gertrude resolved to observe her rule with the greatest possible fidelity. How could she be indifferent when she saw others whose conduct was tending to destroy religious life?[1]

Gertrude in her zeal for regular life, sometimes ventured to reprove even persons renowned for their virtues. One of the nuns asked Christ to moderate this ardor for fear it would give scandal. "I acted so when I was on earth," he told her. "She resembles me in that. Some of the Jews were regarded as the holiest of men and yet they were scandalized by me."

On a Septuagesima Sunday, when the words, *Ubi est frater tuus Abel?* were chanted, Gertrude understood that God will hold each religious responsible for the faults against the rule which she could have prevented by timely correction. The excuse that some give, "It is not my duty

[1] One or two German writers who wish to make St. Gertrude a precursor of the Protestant Reformation have interpreted this passage to refer to religion in general. The saint's resolution to obey her rule faithfully indicates however that the reference is to the *state* of religion, that is, conventual or monastic life.

to correct him," or "I am worse than he," will be no more acceptable than Cain's words, "Am I my brother's keeper?"

Discretion not permitting her to do otherwise, the saint sought the correction of the faults of her superiors only by recommending them to God. As she did this, she learned that submission to imperfect superiors is more meritorious than to the irreproachable. Similarly, superiors profit by the defects as well as by the virtues of their communities.

THE WOMAN

As a result of her efforts, Gertrude encountered skepticism and hostility. Even among holy and intelligent women there are differences of temperament, and her companions did not find her faultless. It has already been observed that some of them thought her too severe in her admonitions. In her writings Gertrude mentions detractions and even calumnies but does not reveal their nature.

The saint sometimes found herself in a dilemma caused by her zeal for God's glory on the one hand, and on the other, by her unwillingness to outrage members of the community who might find her too insistent on minor observances. She offered to the Savior the pain that she foresaw as a result of her actions and received the comforting reply: "Every time that you incur a reproach for my love, I shall fortify you as a city is surrounded by walls and moats in order that no occupation may ever distract or separate you from me. Moreover, I shall give you the merits that each sister would have acquired by submitting humbly to your remonstrances for my glory."

On another occasion he reminded her that the virtue of concord is not destroyed when men oppose injustice. One gets the impression that some rigorous persons found in her gifts a pretext for resentment rather than a source of edification; indeed, her contemporary biographer hints as much.

Gertrude's zeal for justice and her freedom from human respect would not necessarily have been appreciated by all her companions. One of her contemporaries writes: "She would not have defended by a single word her dearest friend even against her own enemy if by so doing she might be guilty of injustice. In fact, if justice demanded it, she would condemn her own mother rather than commit the least injustice even to an enemy."

This devotion to justice cost her dearly since she loved and esteemed all her sisters. Yet she had no illusions about their shortcomings, and once with engaging candor asked Christ why her frequent prayers for her friends apparently had so little effect. He answered her by a similitude: "When a young prince returns from the emperor's palace where he has been invested with great possessions, those who meet him see only the weakness of childhood and are unaware how powerful he will become. Then do not be astonished if you see no effect from your prayers. My eternal wisdom disposes of them to greater advantage. The more one prays for another, the happier that person will be. Persevering prayer is never without fruit although men on earth do not know in what way it will be answered."

On another occasion Christ said to her: "Anyone who loves and defends the truth and thereby loses his friends, undergoes suffering, or performs great labor, that person like Mary Magdalen, breaks the alabaster vase and pours on my head a precious perfume which fills the house with its fragrance. Such a one gives good example, and while correcting the faults of others, he also corrects his own

131

since he will avoid committing those for which he blames his neighbor." Yet Gertrude would not have been human if she had not felt averse to reproving others. "Lord," she once asked, "why must I be the scourge of your friends?"

In addition to these trials Gertrude likewise suffered with her sisters from various troubles which beset the entire community (See Book I, Chapter I). Although several threatened assaults on the monastery had been prevented by the prayers of the nuns, nevertheless many other trials beset them. The convent had been robbed more than once, and it was only natural that the sisters should feel some bitterness toward their enemies. Gertrude herself was not free from this feeling of resentment. It is one thing to forgive an isolated injury and another to go on forgiving when the injury is repeated. Christ appeared to her with his arm painfully wounded, saying: "Think what I should suffer if someone should strike me cruelly on this injured arm. I am so treated by those who have no pity for the risk of damnation incurred by your persecutors, and who publish the wrongs and damages you suffer, forgetting that these evil-doers are also my members. On the other hand, those who are compassionate and who implore my mercy that these sinners may be converted, apply a soothing ointment to my arm. And whoever by wise counsel leads them to the amendment of their lives resembles a skillful physician who restores the arm to its normal state."

Gertrude was amazed. "Merciful Lord!" she exclaimed, "how can you call such unworthy persons your arm? They have been cut off from the body of the Church, publicly excommunicated because of the disturbance they have caused in our monastery." "Nevertheless," said Christ, "since they can be reunited to the Church through absolution I must take care of them. I desire with incredible ardor that they be converted and restored to me through penitence." As Gertrude, with understandable insistence resumed her prayer for the protection of her convent, Christ continued: "If you humiliate yourselves under my mighty hand and acknowledge that you have deserved these punishments, my fatherly mercy will preserve you from all hostile invasion; but if you rise up proudly against your persecutors, wishing to return evil for evil, then by my just decree I shall allow them to prevail against you and do you even more harm." (The reference to excommunication suggests that these enemies were under the leadership of Gebhardt, who had already attacked the monastery in 1294. Elsewhere, however, it is said that the convent had many enemies.)

It has been mentioned that the monastery was sometimes burdened with debts. The persons in charge of temporal affairs felt the greatest anxiety, but Gertrude also entered sympathetically into their difficulties. The urgency with which creditors pressed their claims provided her with a forceful comparison in her *Exercises:* "Already the creditor is at the door, reclaiming from me the trust of life, exacting a return proportioned to the time which has been given me. If I parley with him I am undone, for I have not wherewithal to pay what I owe."

While Gertrude prayed insistently that the convent officials might be enabled to pay the debt in order that they might have more time to pray and fewer distractions, Christ told her: "It does not matter to me whether you perform spiritual exercises or manual labor, provided only that your will is directed to me with a right intention. If I took pleasure only in your spiritual exercises, I should certainly have reformed human nature after Adam's fall so

133

that it would not need food, clothing, or the other things that man must find or make with such effort.

"A mighty emperor is not contented merely to have ladies-in-waiting richly attired in his palace, but he has also men-at-arms, officials fit for various services and always ready to carry out his orders. So I do not find my pleasure merely in the interior exercise of contemplation, but also in various exterior and useful works which are directed to my honor; these too invite me to live among the children of men and find my delight in them. Furthermore it is by manual works that men find occasion to practice charity, patience, humility, and other virtues." Gertrude then saw the chief procurator of the monastery offering to God with great difficulty a piece of gold set with a precious jewel. Christ said to her: "If I lessened his troubles as you ask, I should be deprived of that jewel which pleases me so much, and he would lose the reward prepared for him."

Gertrude's faults—impetuosity and impatience—were those natural to an ardent temperament. Another trait was her apparent absent-mindednes. During the chanting of the office she was sometimes so lost in God that she did not know whether the other sisters were sitting or standing, and had to have her attention called to her surroundings. Such abstraction is likely to cause amusement or annoyance. Gertrude asked the Lord to withdraw his special favors during the time of community prayers in order that she might not neglect the rubrics. Instead, he enabled her to remain in a state of contemplation while conforming perfectly to the actions of the rest of the community.

However vehement the accusations of others, they were mild compared to Gertrude's self-indictments. She charges herself with "malicious lightness, passionate words and actions, worldly conversations, squandering the talent of time, and misusing God's gifts." Although in her intercourse with Christ she shows the most profound reverence, yet she sees herself as guilty of "boorish ignorance and discourtesy."

In her fourth *Exercise* she prays to be delivered from "timidity of spirit and from storminess, from all perversity of heart and from fleshliness, from all heedlessness in my behavior. . . ." She asked St. Mechtild to pray for patience and meekness for her; and indeed impatience is evidently her most persistent fault. Sometimes it was caused by depression or by the neglect of those who took care of her in her illness. It may well be that the depression was a symptom of the disease, apparently hepatitis, which eventually caused her death. Her disquiet when no one came to take her to the chapel is surely understandable. Nearly always the movements of impatience were interior and did not find expression in words.

She often accuses herself of negligence in general. Once she mentions carelessness in pronouncing the words of the office and in dismissing useless thoughts. She believes that she has been an obstacle to her friends by depending on them instead of on God alone. Failure to thank him for his favors, failure to rejoice with her sisters and to sympathize with them in times of sorrow—these are also cited in her self-denunciation.

It is hard for readers of her works to believe that Gertrude was often guilty of these lapses. Of those making progress in the way of perfection it has been said, that "because of their fervent desire to fulfill faithfully all their obligations and because of their peculiar psychological state of recollection in God, they may sometimes be inadvertently careless, forgetful of certain details, and perhaps even commit certain faults which they cannot correct, no matter how strenuously they try. These things are an abundant source of complaints and severe reprimands and cause souls to suffer keenly, for they judge themselves culpable but find that they are helpless to remedy their light imperfections."[2]

THE SAINT

It would be wrong to conclude that Gertrude's life was a triumphal progress, that she was invariably loved and esteemed. She was sometimes hurt by the ingratitude of her friends, sometimes neglected in her illness. Occasionally she was unable to get to the chapel because no one came to assist her. It pained her that sometimes her words were without effect. Often after she had spoken decisively to someone, she doubted the correctness of what she had said, especially when she had urged a timorous person to receive holy communion. Christ repeatedly assured her, however, that he had spoken in her and that she should be confident of his direction when she gave advice to others.

A particularly grievous trial was the temporary loss of her gift of gracious speech and eloquent instruction. When this occurred, Christ said to her: "If you still had the gift of eloquence you would perhaps attribute to it the facility with which you draw souls to me. I have withdrawn it in part to teach you that your power comes from me, and that I have given it to you by a special grace."

In all the vicissitudes of the monastery Gertrude shared fully. She entered whole-heartedly into community life with its joys and sorrows. Apropos of the saint's love for her sisters, her biographer, quoting St. Gregory, declares that sanctity consists not in working miracles but rather in loving one's neighbors as oneself. In the *Legatus,* the importance of mutual support is illustrated by the image of a

[2] Arintero, *The Mystical Evolution in the Development and Vitality of the Church,* II, 108.

wall made of precious stones held together by the gold of charity. Indeed, Gertrude esteemed her sisters so much that she was accustomed to seek favors from God by reminding him of the goodness of her companions.

Her solicitude for the welfare of her neighbors extended also to their temporal needs. Although Gertrude apparently had not the strength for heavy physical labor, she was not indifferent to the burdens of others in the household, but often sympathized with them and prayed for them. It has already been noted that she was particularly concerned for those who kept the monastery accounts and were in financial difficulties.

Even for a person in good health, such unremitting labor as Gertrude took on herself would have been taxing, and she was not robust. Serious illness sometimes prevented her from taking part in the community exercises; sometimes she could remain for only part of the office. During an entire year she was absent from the choral chant.

When it was impossible for her to take an active part in the prayers of the community, Gertrude would go to the choir and sit there during the chanting of the office so that she might use what little strength she had in the service of God. It grieved her that on such occasions she lacked fervor and could scarcely pronounce a few words or chant several notes. Christ comforted her by saying that every word and every neum chanted in his honor afforded him more pleasure than she would feel if a friend gave her a delicious and strengthening drink of new mead. Similarly, when she wondered whether she should stand at the Gospel though she felt unable to do so, he told her: "When you accomplish something that exceeds your strength, I accept it as indispensable to my honor; but when you omit anything with a right intention, I accept those omissions as if I myself were infirm. Thus I reward both man-

137

ners of acting according to my divine magnanimity." Gertrude received a special illumination on this matter when the words *Gloriosum sanguinem* were sung on the feast of some martyrs. She then reflected that just as blood which in itself inspires horror is praised when it is poured forth for the honor of God, so when religious duties are omitted for reasons of charity or obedience, these omissions are pleasing to God and therefore praiseworthy.

Far from cutting her off from the liturgical cycle, Gertrude's illnesses were the occasion for many illuminations concerning the mysteries of Christ's life. In her wakeful nights she was honored by special visitations of divine grace. Christ encouraged her in her sufferings, particularly when the other sisters were too busy to attend to her wants: "My child," he said, "you are always with me, and all I have is yours." Once he showed her, under the form of two jeweled rings which he wore, the pleasures and pains that she had offered him. Again, he touched her left eye with the ring which represented physical suffering, and from that time, she felt extreme pain in that eye.

Once when, despite her great weakness, Gertrude had risen to recite Matins and had already completed the first nocturn, she recommenced it in order to say it with a young sister. (Evidently this was one of the many times when the saint's infirmities prevented her from chanting office with the community; the other sister was no doubt also ill.) Christ was pleased by Gertrude's unselfishness and revealed to her that he had adorned her spiritually with a jewel for each word she had repeated.

Gertrude's poor health did not deter her from offering to go with a group of sisters to make a new foundation when the emissaries of a certain nobleman requested this. Yet soon remembering that she had hardly strength enough for her duties at Helfta, she considered herself foolish to desire this mission. Christ nevertheless showed himself pleased by her good desires "as if an ointment had been applied to his wounds." The contemporary biographer says that whatever God permitted seemed right to Gertrude; the fact that the proposed foundation was never made did not disturb her. Her attitude recalls St. Bernard's saying, "Whom God pleases, he pleases God."

From all these experiences Gertrude developed the conviction so admirably expressed in the words: "Adversity is the ring by which the soul is espoused to Christ." Yet it should be noted that she took remedies in her illness, and that at least once, exhausted by the importunities of her sisters and guests, she went to bed to escape them.

THE FRIEND

Sharing the common life at Helfta, St. Gertrude and St. Mechtild reacted similarly to the trials and sorrows of the community: the interdict imposed by the canons of Halberstadt, the drought which endangered their harvests, the pressure of debt, the fear of marauding armies, especially in 1294 during the war between the Emperor Adolph and the sons of Albert of Saxony. Likewise, the death of the good Abbess Gertrude is recorded with grief by both Gertrude and Mechtild. The latter had the additional sorrow of being prevented by illness from attending her sister; Gertrude, as substitute chantress, intoned the antiphon, *"Surge Virgo"* at the deathbed of the abbess.

The names of Gertrude and Mechtild are inseparably linked in the history of mysticism. In fact, their lives and their writings are so closely related that the Solesmes editors speak of Gertrude's *Legatus Divinae Pietatis* and Mechtild's *Liber Specialis Gratiae* as blood relatives.

In social rank, however, the two saints were widely separated: Gertrude, as has previously been noted, was a nameless orphan, while Mechtild was a member of one of the most illustrious families of the region, the barons of Hackeborn and lords of Wippra, who were benefactors of the community from the time of its foundation.

Although St. Gertrude and St. Mechtild were not sisters, as the older biographers mistakenly assert, they were united in the most profound and spiritual relationship. Equals in the timeless world of the spirit, despite their difference in age and rank, they rejoiced in a friendship rooted in the love of God. Furthermore, although St. Gertrude regarded sentimental friendship as "a deadly poison," and would decline even the most helpful services if she believed that she was being given what was God's by right, she found, with St. Mechtild, there was no such danger.

Their love of music was also a bond between the two friends. Gertrude, as we have seen, sometimes substituted for Mechtild as chantress. One of her amusing comparisons refers to the displeasure felt by a person with a good voice *(multum sonoram et valde flexibilem)* if someone with a poor voice *(valde gravem et dissonam)* should insist on taking her place. The chanting of those who have little devotion or who take a purely natural pleasure in singing is compared to heavy and unmelodious chords from a stringed instrument. Gertrude herself loved music so much that she had to be on guard against yielding to a merely human satisfaction in singing.

Moreover, it would appear that St. Gertrude and St. Mechtild had the same type of constitution. Insomnia and chronic illness are reported of both. Both accepted their physical pain as the chastisements of a loving God, and therefore to be received, as Gertrude says, most willingly and joyfully, "for bodily and spiritual sufferings are the sign of the espousal of the soul to God." St. Mechtild had learned that whereas in health one is embraced, as it were, by the right arm of Christ, in sickness it is by his left arm, "which is nearer his Heart."

Gertrude and Mechtild have been called "the saints of the holy humanity of Christ." His incarnation, his divine infancy, the events of his public life, Passion, and death as brought successively to mind through the liturgical cycle, occupied the thoughts and directed the prayers of the saints of Helfta.

Both saw Christ presiding at the conventual chapter on Christmas Eve. Both were particularly devoted to the mystery of the incarnation, to the Holy Face, to the wounds of Christ, to all the episodes of his Passion. Likewise, their divine Master visited both of them in their illness.

Moreover, although Mechtild and Gertrude felt that they were insufficiently devoted to the Mother of God, they received most liberal reassurances that Christ would supply all that was lacking in their devotion to his mother.

In their religious devotions, as we have noted, both Gertrude and Mechtild dedicated themselves to honoring the Holy Face, especially on the second Sunday after Epiphany when the relics of the Passion were venerated at the Vatican basilica. On this day, Gertrude was comforted by Christ's assurance that he would accept her least action—even so slight a one as picking up a straw, speaking a single word, showing a kindness to someone, saying a *Requiem aeternam* for the dead, or offering any prayer for sinners or for the just. He told her, "How affectionately I shall receive anyone who at the end of the year brings me the fruits of his love in number exceeding his sins!" Gertrude was doubtful that anyone could do this, "since man's heart is so prone to evil." "Why should it be so difficult," Christ asked, "since I am pleased by the least sign of zeal and assist it by my omnipotence?"

When reflecting on the divine generosity, Mechtild

141

often said: "If all the good things that have come to me from the most gracious Heart of God were to be written down, the book of Matins would not suffice."

The most significant spiritual relationship existing between Mechtild and Gertrude, however, was that of their devotion to the Sacred Heart. (This devotion will be discussed in another chapter.)

In conclusion, therefore, we note that in their differing roles lies the chief distinction between these two saints of Helfta. The spiritual history of St. Mechtild is well expressed by the title of her book, *The Book of Special Grace.* Her particular mission, marked by graces of a unique and intimate character, was to enlighten and to encourage her young friend to undertake the task of revealing the mysteries of God's love. For herself, her choice was to remain hidden. Although Mechtild was, as we have seen, prominent in the community, nevertheless her long-term mission does not, like Gertrude's, fit into the central stream of the great devotion with which she was so closely associated.

GERTRUDE AND ST. TERESA

In many of her traits St. Gertrude resembles St. Teresa of Avila; she has in fact been called "the Teresa of Germany." In the writings of the Spanish mystic one finds many echoes of St. Gertrude. The literary style of both saints—direct, vivid, and graceful—is a corollary to many resemblances in their spirituality. Both had a special devotion to the Divine Infant, both experienced a mystical wounding of the heart, and both show the perfect balance of contemplation and ardor. The Abbe Guéranger in his preface to St. Gertrude's *Exercises,* quotes Ribera, St Teresa's confessor, as saying that she had taken St. Gertrude as her mistress and guide. While a careful reading of Ribera's life of Teresa does not disclose any such statement, Ribera draws many parallels between the two saints.

The account of Teresa by Fray Ibañez, however, might also be taken as applying to Gertrude as well: "Our Lord has given her great compassion for those about her, knowledge of her own faults, much regard for good persons, and abasement of herself." Diego Yepes, also Teresa's confessor, wrote to Dom Leander, who had translated Gertrude's writings into Spanish: "I hope that his Majesty will grant you the grace that you may be assisted at the hour of your death by his two faithful spouses, who during their lives were always so full of gratitude and courtesy." It was Bishop Yepes who commissioned the painting of St. Gertrude which has been often copied; apparently he also had paintings made of the two saints together.

Both Gertrude and Teresa had contact with members of the Dominican Order, finding in them faithful friends during life and champions after death. The Carmelite Order also has been active in propagating the writings of St. Gertrude. In 1633, the Provincial, Denis of the Mother of God, paraphrasing Dante's tribute to St. Francis and St. Dominic, observed of the two saints, Gertrude and Teresa: "The conformity of spirit between these two saints is so exact that whoever approves of one approves of the other."

Obviously, this resemblance is in the spirit rather than in the vocations of the two saints. They were not called to the same work in their orders. Yet though Gertrude was without the executive ability of the great Carmelite, it is unquestionable that her influence, though hidden, was also powerful and enduring. Never elected to a post as superior, Gertrude nevertheless exercised a leadership far more exalted than that of the noble abbesses of the monastery of Helfta: the first superior, Cunegunde the Godfearing; the competent and motherly Gertrude von Hackeborn; and Catherine von Watzdorff, one of the last abbesses, the target for Luther's attack.

Some Aspects of St. Gertrude's Spirituality: Liturgical and Personal

The spirituality of St. Gertrude is eminently liturgical and therefore eminently Benedictine. Pourrat has observed that almost every word of the office and of the mass furnished her the inspiration for communion with God.[1]

The influence of the Dominicans in the spiritual life at Helfta has already been mentioned. In Gertrude the firm doctrinal formation which this intercourse assured was blended with the traditional Benedictine spirituality —the peace which is the motto of the Benedictine order. With this peace is associated a spirit of poetry and a liberty of spirit to which Father Faber has paid tribute: "No one," he writes, "can be at all acquainted with the old-fashioned Benedictine school of spiritual writers without perceiving and admiring the beautiful liberty of spirit which pervades and possesses their whole mind. It is just what we should expect from an order of such matured traditions. St. Gertrude is a fair specimen of them. She is thoroughly Benedictine. . . . A spirit of breadth, a spirit of liberty, that is

[1] P. Pourrat, La Spiritualité Chrétienne: II, Le Moyen Age (Paris, 1946) p. 2.

the Catholic spirit; and it was eminently the badge of the old Benedictine ascetics."[2]

GERTRUDE AND ST. BERNARD

Also, although she has her own highly individual character, the influence of St. Bernard is clear in many of Gertrude's ideas and expressions. Any discussion of the saint's spirituality must begin by taking account of this influence.

Like St. Bernard, Gertrude "ruminated" the psalms. Her delight in the mystery of the incarnation also resembles his, and his homilies *Super Missus Est* were probably familiar to her. (Lepitre has said, "She teaches admirably the theology of the incarnation.")

Confidence, the lesson taught by the nativity of the incarnate Son, is a virtue of which both Bernard and Gertrude gave special evidence in the hour of their death. Both also had a particular devotion to the name of Jesus. St. Bernard recommended admiration of the virtues of others and consideration of one's own lack of virtue; it has been shown that Gertrude habitually practiced this attitude.

In their writings both saints combine gentleness with vigor. What Gertrude most admired in the *doctor mellifluus* was his gift of persuasive eloquence; it was a gift she shared. Both Bernard and Gertrude employ some daring images in their writings. The chief expression of his mysticism is in his sermons on the *Song of Songs;* Gertrude's mystical relations with Christ have been called a living commentary on these homilies. Pourrat reminds us that the true mystics, being dead to the life of the senses and living only for God ("Leave your bodies outside the

[2] F. W. Faber, *All for Jesus* (London, 1854) p. 354.

monastery," said St. Bernard to those who wished to enter the order) express the force of the divine love that consumes them by the use of some comparisons startling to the uninitiated.[3]

St. Bernard's devotion to our Lady is proverbial; Dante commemorates it in the *Paradiso*. It was Bernard who added to the *Salve Regina* the words, *"O clemens, O pia, O dulcis Maria"; (virgo* is a later addition). He popularized the idea of Mary as distributor of graces, a concept also found in Gertrude's writings.

The chief point of resemblance between the saint of Helfta and St. Bernard, her spiritual father, lies, however, in their recognition that identification of the spirit of Christ with the spirit of man through love renders all common between them. Bernard's words are: "All things are common to them . . . one home, one table, one bed." *(Quibus omnia communia sunt . . . Una domus, una mensa, unus thorus.* Sermon VII, 2; Sermon XXIII, 12, 15, 16) As Ruysbroek explains, "When I say we are one with God, it must be understood that I speak of love, not of the essence or of the nature." Both to Bernard and to Gertrude as to other mystics, the expression, "the kiss of the spouse," means the possession of God which is the essence of the mystical union. It is most important to remember this.

A dissimilarity between the two saints is in their attitude toward nature. Gertrude's appreciation of the landscape of Helfta is one of the first traits to attract a modern reader. Unlike the German mystics of the following century, she resembles St. Francis of Assisi in her love of nature through which she contemplated God, as the famous "courtyard passage" in Book Two of the *Legatus* illustrates. Bernard's indifference to natural beauty is perpetuated in

[3] Pourrat, p. 98, note 1.

the well-known anecdote of his passing the lake of Lausanne while remaining completely unaware of it. His apparent abstraction might be better understood, however, not as contempt of nature but rather as evidence of deep recollection; he was equally unaware of what he was eating or drinking.

SPIRITUAL INFLUENCES FROM THE BIBLE

In addition to the example of St. Bernard, Gertrude also found many parallels between her interior life and the lives of certain personages in the Bible. She was particularly attracted to Esther, the Hebrew queen. Her treatise on Esther, now lost, began with the words, *"Egredimini, filiae Jerusalem,"* a text later associated with the feast of the Sacred Heart. Once, in preparation for the feast of the Ascension, Gertrude implored Christ to pardon her sins and negligences. At that time, he likened her to the beautiful Esther, saying, "Ask what you will and I shall give it to you." In her role of second Esther, Gertrude acted as intercessor for all the members of the Church and was graciously heard by Christ, "the true Assuerus," who opened to her the treasury of his Sacred Heart. It seemed to her that the nun who led the prayers at the chanting of the office also fulfilled the mission of Esther in praying for her people, that is, for her community.

Whereas Esther used diplomacy and her queenly power to outwit the enemies of her people, Gertrude dealt with persecutors by praying for them. For all those who afflicted the community she asked the grace of repentance. On one occasion the saint was so oppressed by the sense of her unworthiness and weakness that she could not follow her custom of praising God and aspiring to contemplation. All at once it seemed to her that, clothed in the beauty that had adorned Esther before Assuerus, she was presented to the King of kings. Greeting her as Lady and Queen, Christ asked her, "What do you wish?" She answered, "I ask and desire with all my heart that your adorable will may be wholly accomplished in me." He then named to her the various persons who had been recommended to her prayers, asking what she desired for each. Her courage restored by the communication of the merits of Christ, the saint said, "For them also I desire the same as for myself; and that your loving and peaceable will may be fulfilled in every creature, I should willingly submit every member of my body to punishment." Each parallel between herself and the beautiful Jewish queen, however, served only to humble Gertrude in her own eyes and make her more uneasy at being revered by her companions.

Many other scriptural episodes and phrases are woven into the record of Gertrude's spiritual life. When she felt unworthy to receive communion and realized that even if she spent a thousand years she could not make herself fit for union with Christ, she adapted the parable of the Prodigal Son to her own situation. She took courage, knowing that if she approached the Savior with humility, he would perceive her "while she was yet afar off," and clothe her with the garments and jewels of his own innocence, love, humility, hope, and confidence. Again, in expressing her desire for death and her confidence in the grace of God, she paraphrased the words of Psalm 17 and linked them with those of St. Paul, "In thee, O God my Lover, I shall leap over the wall of the body and find myself in that place of security and of rejoicing where I shall behold thee no longer in a dark manner but in truth and face to face."

St. Gertrude's many gospel quotations are chiefly from those of St. John and St. Matthew. She likewise takes many texts from the epistles of St. Paul and several from the

Apocalypse. A number of the passages she quotes or paraphrases are from the liturgy, which might also have suggested to her the linking of passages from the Old and the New Testament as illustrated above.

GERTRUDE AND THE LITURGY

St. Gertrude's meditations on the details of Christ's temporal life were sustained by the liturgy in which that life is perpetually reenacted. Today when emphasis on liturgy has made some persons uneasy about their preference for private prayer, it is reassuring to see that Gertrude's practice fused the two. True to the spirit of her order, she gave first place to the mass. More than once Gertrude saw Christ in priestly or pontifical garments; and on one occasion when she was unable to go to the community mass, she assisted spiritually at a mass of which he was the celebrant. A choir of angels attended, and other angels were the servers.

At every part of the holy sacrifice she received a special communication of divine grace—for example, at the Kyrie she obtained the forgiveness of all her sins of frailty and ignorance. As the mass proceeded, she gave some of the responses: Christ intoned *"Dominus vobiscum, dilecta,"* and she answered, *"Et cum spiritu tuo, Praedilecte!"* St. John the Evangelist chanted the epistle and another evangelist the gospel. During the offertory, the saints and angels presented to Christ a golden chalice containing all the sufferings of soul and body which she had endured from her infancy. Our Lady sang the Sanctus. When the bell in the monastery church rang for the elevation there, Christ lifted his Sacred Heart, immolating it to his Eternal Father.

Throughout the mass, Gertrude prayed for the entire Church, while offering all her own prayers, works, and sufferings with contrition for her sins. She recited the

Credo in the name of the Church. At the offertory, the Heart of Christ appeared under the form of a golden altar on which the guardian angels laid the works and prayers of those committed to their charge. The divine celebrant himself gave her the host at the time for communion. This occurred on Gaudete Sunday.

On another occasion, Christ taught her how to assist spiritually at mass by suggesting five subjects for meditation, each of which would serve for one part of the mass. She learned also that when anyone devoutly attends mass, he is purified of sin, beautifully clothed with the merits of Christ, and regarded by God the Father with the same pleasure with which he beholds the consecrated host.

The divine office, the *opus Dei*, was second only to the mass in St. Gertrude's devotions. At the Invitatory on Easter Sunday, as she was thinking of the frequent use of the word Alleluia, Christ said to her: "You can praise me worthily by uniting your homage with that which the heavenly court offers me through this word. Notice that in the Alleluia, you find all the vowels except 'o', which signifies sorrow." As Gertrude continued her recitation of the office, Christ enabled her to understand each verse in relation to the feast of Easter. This is the grace signified by the words, "Sing to the Lord a new song," since he enlightens his friends to perceive hidden meanings even in words that they have sung daily for many years.

THE EUCHARIST

Devotion to the Holy Eucharist became intense and widespread during the thirteenth century. For Gertrude, appreciation of the sacrament was of course inseparable from her appreciation of the sacrifice of the mass. She was taught by Christ that no number of individual prayers and penances can approach in value the offering of his own body and blood to his Eternal Father. It is like gold, which united to the silver of humanity forms a precious amalgam. Once, when after having planned to abstain from communion, Gertrude was so drawn by the grace of God that she received the blessed sacrament, Christ said to her: "Today by your own will you were going to render me only the service of one who brings to his master mortar, bricks, and straw; but in my love I have chosen you and placed you among the joyful banqueters who feast at my table."

When a sermon on justice had so terrified her that she feared to receive communion, the saint heard Christ say, "Look at the narrow vessel in which I am enclosed, and know that the rigor of my justice is thus limited by the mercy that I show men in this sacrament." On a similar occasion she was encouraged by these words: "See the smallness of the form beneath which I hide myself to nourish you with my divinity and my humanity, and compare it with the proportions of the human body. Just as the human body exceeds in size the form beneath which I hide my body, so my love and mercy induce me to allow the human soul to show itself, so to speak, more powerful than I."

That humility is more pleasing to God than sensible devotion was made clear to Gertrude once when she felt insufficiently prepared to receive the sacrament. Seeing a sister approach holy communion with a reverence which was almost fear, Gertrude disapproved of her. Christ, however, rebuked the saint, saying: "Do you not know that respect and honor are due me as well as love? Since human frailty cannot offer this double homage at once, and since you are all members of one body, let each by her own disposition compensate for what the others lack."

The custom of elevating the host immediately after the consecration became general before the end of the thirteenth century. To look upon the host was regarded as a great privilege, and in England especially, a number of "Welcome prayers" were composed to greet Christ in the sacramental species at the moment of the elevation. Typical prayers began "Welcome, Lord, in form of bread," or "Jesu Lord, welcome thou be/In form of bread as I thee see."

Like her contemporaries, Gertrude loved to look at the consecrated host. She had learned that every longing and reverent glance at the blessed sacrament brings an increase of merit and a special reward in heaven. Once, however, when the number of people prevented her from looking at the host, Christ said to her, "If you would know delight, approach. It is not by seeing but by tasting that you will perceive the sweetness of the hidden manna."

Despite the fact that the hosts used in the masses at Helfta were large and thick, it once happened that the dropping of a host passed unnoticed by the celebrant and the sisters. It was not discovered until the sacristan was folding the altar linens. Gertrude knew by divine revelation that the host had not been consecrated; nevertheless, she did not say so, desiring that Christ might not be deprived of the honor of reparation.

At a time when it was not the custom to communicate daily, the saint urged her sisters to receive communion frequently, and often brought peace of mind to those whom scruples prevented from approaching the sacrament.

In addition to the doubts which many of the nuns felt about the propriety of receiving communion often, they were also exposed to the vehemence of someone designated only as "a certain person." Carried away by zeal, she used to exclaim against those who, she felt, received communion with too little preparation or devotion. She even reproached the nuns and frightened some of them away from the sacrament.

Gertrude, troubled by this behavior, asked the Lord about it and received the touching answer: "My delights are to be with the children of men, and in my excelling love I have left them this sacrament that they might remember me. I have promised to remain with my faithful ones in this sacrament till the end of time. Whoever keeps from communion someone who is not in a state of mortal sin, hinders or interrupts the delight that I take in that soul. She resembles a harsh tutor who forbids a king's son the delightful companionship of children his own age if they are poor or not of noble rank. He thinks it more fitting that the child should enjoy royal honors than that he should play ball in the street."

"But," Gertrude asked, "if this person resolved not to give such advice in the future, would you not pardon her?" Christ's answer was reassuring: "I should not only pardon her," he said, "but I should find as much pleasure in her action as the king's son would feel if his tutor restored to him the companionship of those children whom he had driven away."

Once when many of the sisters were abstaining from communion "for various reasons," she thanked God for having placed her in such a situation that neither relatives nor any other consideration could keep her from the divine banquet. This is a mysterious remark. How could relatives keep a sister from holy communion? Did misplaced feelings of family loyalty induce them to forego the sacrament when their relatives were under ecclesiastical censure? (We have already noted that many of the nuns were related to the local nobility.) Our Lord's words to Gertrude indicate that this may have been the reason. He said, "Learn that there is nothing in heaven or earth, not even my justice and my judgments that can hinder the benefits that my divine heart desires to grant you." On another occasion, during the time of the interdict when the sisters could not receive the sacrament, she saw Christ spiritually entering into communion with each one.

Gertrude's own preparation for holy communion included special watchfulness against sins committed by the tongue. "A person who receives communion after sins of speech is like one who invites a guest and then heaps up a great pile of stones at the door."

The saint's desire for the blessed sacrament was so strong that she would have forced her way to it through drawn swords. While she watched the other nuns receiving communion, it seemed to her that it was not the priest but Christ who was giving himself, the priest merely making the sign of the cross over each host.

One of the most striking expressions of Christ's indwelling occurred when at the time of communion he said to Gertrude: "I will clothe myself with you that I may be able to extend my hand to sinners. . . . And I will also clothe you with myself in order that all those for whom you pray and those who by nature are like you may be made worthy to receive my innumerable benefits."

It was immediately after communion that the saint experienced the fulfillment of the request, "Water of Christ's side, wash me," in the prayer *Anima Christi*. A life-giving tide seemed to flow over her spirit, not only cleansing it, but transforming it from a withered branch into a fruitful tree.

It was also after communion that she received the wound of divine love. "The demonstrations of earthly love," Christ told her, "can give no idea of the joys imparted by this sacramental union. For the delights of human love are passing, but the sweetness of this union can never diminish; on the contrary, it increases with every renewal."

As a preparation for holy communion, Gertrude was accustomed to meditate on the hymn, *Jesu nostra Redemptio.* She would also pray to our Lady and the saints that she might offer to God all the admirable dispositions with which they had received his graces. When she asked Christ to offer to his Father the perfection that had been his on the day of his ascension, he told her, "In the eyes of the heavenly court you appear robed in all the merits that you desire." Then he added, "Is it so hard for you to believe that I can accomplish this? Does not one who wishes to honor his friend clothe him in his own garments?" When she prayed for those who had been recommended to her, Christ said, "I shall grant them the grace you ask, but it depends on their free will to make use of it."

The advantages of frequent communion formed the subject of one of the saint's meditations. Understanding that Christ gave her through the reception of the sacrament the entire gift of himself even as he had given himself to his Blessed Mother, she asked, "What advantage have I over those who received you when I did yesterday and do not do so today?" Christ answered, "Among the ancients you know that one who had been elected a second time to the consulate was more honored than one elected only a single time. Why then should the soul more frequently united to me not receive a greater glory?"

As Gertrude sighed with envy of priests who may communicate daily, he said to her: "It is certain that marvelous glory is destined for those who receive me worthily. But do not confuse the love of the soul at the time of communion with the glory attached to the celebration of the sacred mysteries." She learned that there are various rewards: "one for the heart burning with love and desires; another

156

for the one who receives me with love and reverence; and still another for one who makes a long and fervent preparation to receive me. None of these gifts are for a priest who celebrates through routine and without fervor."

Sometimes Gertrude's illness not only deprived her of physical strength but kept her from making her usual preparation for holy communion. Nevertheless, though she felt unprepared, her longing was so intense that she exclaimed: "Sweetness of my soul, I know how unworthy I am to receive your body and blood, and I should abstain today from holy communion if I could find relief and consolation in any creature whatsoever. But from the east to the west, from the north to the south, there is no one but you who can give joy and refreshment to my body and soul. Behold me now, filled with love and breathless with desire, I run to the fountain of life."

In response, Christ made her understand that he found in her a unique pleasure. As she doubted that this could be true of one so unworthy, she learned that it was his own numerous and beautiful gifts that made her pleasing in God's sight. It became her conviction that every spiritual loss can be repaired by worthily receiving the body and blood of Christ; as a result, she never became unduly depressed by her faults.

That this confidence which is the special mark of Gertrude's spirituality was not second nature to her becomes clear as we read of the many lessons she received in conquering timidity and mistrust. When in response to her exclamation that she was poor and unworthy to approach the eucharistic banquet, Christ cleansed her through the merits of his Passion and adorned her with radiant jewels taken from his own person, he counseled her to walk with the dignity that becomes one so appareled. She understood that they behave like fools who after receiving the bounty of God remain as small-minded and fearful as before.

That her last nourishment on earth might be the blessed sacrament was one of Gertrude's dearest hopes. Christ gave her to understand, however, that this desire was not to her greatest advantage. Her comment after a dangerous fall proves that she had learned this lesson well. When her sisters asked her how she could express regret that this accident had not caused her death, since in such an event she could not have received the last sacraments, she answered: "I wish with my whole heart to be strengthened by these health-giving sacraments; nevertheless, the will and appointment of God seem to be the best and surest preparation. I am certain that whatever the manner of my death, sudden or foreseen, I shall never lack his mercy, without which I cannot possibly be saved in either case."

She had also learned that the effect of the sacrament received by a sick person is not diminished by the taking of food or drink if the patient's motive be to prolong life for the glory of God. After the reception of the body of Christ, every act accomplished with a good intention is meritorious: to suffer patiently, to eat or drink, all increase the eternal reward by virtue of the continued union of the person with Christ.

When illness prevented her from receiving communion, St. Gertrude was taught that Christ was, as it were, refreshed by the preparation she had made through her guard over her senses, her moderation in speech, her desires and her prayers. Longing to be purified that she might make a spiritual communion, she saw that Christ looked upon her with a glance which resembled the radiance of the sun and produced effects comparable to it. As the sun whitens, softens, and causes fruitfulness, so the look of Christ purifies, melts, and causes the soul to bring forth the flowers and fruits of virtue.

On various feasts Gertrude perceived that the glory of a saint in heaven is augmented by the communions received in his honor. The saints take special delight, she was told on the feast of St. Paul, in one who has made a fervent communion, praising her "even as a bride is congratulated on the day of her nuptials."

Yet feastdays and communions were not invariably joyous occasions for Gertrude. It was a common experience for her to be without consolation at the time of even great feasts of the Church. "This has not happened by chance," said Christ to the saint, "but by a particular providence which inspires feelings of devotion at unexpected times to elevate the heart of man which is so enslaved by the body; but on festivals and at the time of communion I withdraw this grace, preferring to occupy the hearts of my elect with good desires of humility; and this may be more advantageous to them than the grace of devotion."

The biographer of the saint declares that when the presence of Christ was thus withdrawn, Gertrude never fell into depression. To serve Christ with faith, reverence, and gratitude when deprived of devotion is, she realized, to serve him at one's own expense—"like a grandee who serves his king without hire," as St. Teresa puts it.

THE MYSTICAL BODY

From her devotion to the Holy Eucharist Gertrude gradually became more aware of the Mystical Body, and this is the subject of one of her most memorable visions (as it was with the later mystic, Anne Catherine Emmerich). In this vision Christ revealed himself in physical form to Gertrude to show her the reality of his Mystical Body, the Church. His right side was covered with magnificent regal garments, but his entire left side was bare and terribly wounded. The right side represented those who belong to the Church and have been preserved by special grace and by their personal merits. The left side represented the imperfect, still weighed down by their vices and defects. The ornaments on the right side signified the homage and spiritual benefits which some persons by a particular devotion offer to those whom they see excelling themselves in virtue and in the gifts of God; for to honor God's gifts in others is to add an adornment to him.

On the other hand, there are those who willingly perform services for the good, but show such bitter zeal toward the imperfect and wicked that they aggravate instead of correcting the fault. Such persons seem to strike with their fists the wounds of the Mystical Body, and disfigure their own faces with the blood that spurts from these wounds. Nevertheless, the Savior, moved by love for them, behaves as if he had not observed their actions. He pays heed rather to the benefits received by his friends, and with his royal vestments he wipes away the stains from the faces of the others. He said to Gertrude: "Let them learn how to heal the ulcers of my body; that is, to correct their neighbors' faults. They should touch them gently by charitable admonitions. Then if these methods do not succeed, they must resort to more stringent ones.

"But some of them have no care for my wounds; they know their neighbor's defects and scorn him because of them, yet they will not utter a single word for fear of bringing trouble upon themselves. With Cain they ask, 'Am I my brother's keeper?' These persons appear to spread an ointment upon my wounds, but it inflames and infects instead of healing; under cover of silence they allow their neighbor's faults to grow worse when by their words they might have corrected them.

"Others point out his faults to their neighbor, but not seeing immediate improvement, they are outraged and resolve never to advise anyone in the future since their words are not heeded. Yet they will not hesitate secretly to condemn others and even to injure by detraction, without giving a single word of counsel or reproof. These also seem to anoint my wounds, whereas they are at the same time tearing them with burning irons.

"Some refrain from correcting others not so much from malice as from indifference; these persons tread upon my feet. Some care for nothing but their own will; it does not matter to them that they may scandalize my chosen ones, provided that all goes according to their own preference; these pierce my hands with flaming awls.

"Some love and venerate good clergymen, and as is right, praise their words and actions; by so doing they adorn my right side with jeweled ornaments and pearls. Yet these same people are rigorous in their judgment of those who do not keep their rule or who have many faults; by this behavior they shower merciless blows upon my lacerated left side, which I desire them to support with kindness.

"Others actually applaud the ill deeds of prelates and superiors in order to win their favor and permission to do what they please; these turn my head violently and cause me extreme anguish—worse, they insult me in my sufferings and seem to mock at the wounds that cover my face." This impressive image of the Mystical Body is a more extended comparison than the earlier one in which Christ showed St. Gertrude his injured arm as a figure of the persecutors of the community and reproved those who spoke maliciously of them instead of compassionating them and praying for their amendment.[4]

DEVOTION TO MARY

St. Gertrude's devotion to the Mystical Body cannot be dissociated from her devotion to Mary, mother of the Mystical Body.

In the saint's writings, the numerous references to Mary show her under three aspects: first, Mary is active, earnestly interceding for human beings but also ardently praising, thanking, and adoring God; second, she is constantly receiving honors from saints on earth and in heaven; and most of all from her divine Son, who shows her every mark of love and respect; and third, she not only helps men, including sinners, but in imitation of her Son, she shares freely with them all that she has received. St. Gertrude's first reference to our Lady occurs in the second sentence of the *Legatus* in the account of her conversion which, as she says, took place "on the Monday before the feast of the Purification of thy most chaste mother, in a happy hour. . . . " It was in anticipation of the feast of the Annunciation that the saint endeavored to prepare herself for the grace of continued union with God, a grace which was granted her on the vigil of the feast, during chapter. Again, on the feast of the Purification when Gertrude feared that illness would prevent her from receiving communion, our Lady, "the august mediatrix," consoled her by saying that as she had never experienced more severe sufferings than she was then enduring, so had she never received more splendid spiritual gifts than she

---

[4] In the *Lux Fluens Divinitatis* of Mechtild von Magdeburg, Christianity is personified as a poor maiden, half-blind and crippled, with deformed hands and unhealthy skin. She is to be cleansed and cured by the blood of Christ.

was about to receive, and that her physical pain was intended to fortify her soul for the reception of these graces.

On Christmas day, when the words, "She brought forth her first-born Son," were read in the gospel, the saint, asking to be clothed in his own garments of innocence and love, received the Christchild from his mother's hands. Yet Gertrude felt that she had not worthily cared for the divine Infant when, on the succeeding feast of the Purification, his mother appeared to her with a severe countenance, and desired the return of her Son. Recalling Mary's titles, "Reconciliation of Sinners," and "Hope of the Desperate," St. Gertrude reminded her of her role as mother of the fount of forgiveness, and was soon consoled by seeing a compassionate smile on the Blessed Virgin's face. Since a few words had been enough to end her displeasure, the saint felt more than ever convinced that Mary was indeed the mediatrix of the Sacred Heart. When she meditated on the humility and charity of Christ, she thought also of these same virtues in his holy mother, who like him was clothed in garments of green and purple, signifying these qualities. The saint considered as one of God's greatest favors to her that he had given her his mother as her special advocate, recommending her to Mary with the urgent affection of a bridegroom commending his bride to his mother.[5]

The eighth lesson in the office for the feast of the saint refers to the event: *"Deiparam Virginem peculiari beneficio in matrem et procuratricem sibi a Christo datam...."* In the third of her *Exercises* Gertrude asks that she may be

[5] Although both the extant manuscripts of the *Legatus* use the word *dispensatrix* in relating that Christ confided Gertrude to his mother in a special way, Lanspergius the Carthusian has simply said that he gave Mary to St. Gertrude as her mother, obviously changing the text, as the Solesmes editors point out.

presented by Christ to his mother as to her abbess. It is possible that she composed this petition during the interregnum of 1298-1303 when there was no "mother of the monastery."

Gertrude frequently thanked God for the graces conferred on the Blessed Virgin. She praised her as the abode of God and asked that she herself might likewise be honored by his indwelling. With the words, *"Gaude, morum disciplina,"* she acknowledged that Mary had so governed her affections, her desires, and her senses as to offer a perfect homage to her Son. In reply to her prayers, the Blessed Virgin obtained for the saint a share in all these holy dispositions and virtues. The next day, our Lady showed herself under the form of a dazzling white lily with three leaves; on this occasion St. Gertrude composed a prayer, "Hail, white lily of the ever-peaceful and glorious Trinity!" In the sixth of her *Exercises,* she hails Mary as "that virginal rose." The singing of the anthem, *"Stella Maria Maris"* restored her spiritual joy when she was on one occasion overwhelmed with sadness and a tendency to impatience.

Gertrude was taught by Christ to offer the seven canonical hours in praise of the various attributes and dignities of the Blessed Virgin. Once when the saint was saddened by her spiritual poverty, since she had been unable to say even the required prayers and still less able to perform extra works of devotion in preparation for Christmas, Christ offered on her behalf to his holy mother, all the words she had spoken during Advent for the glory of God or the good of others. He added to this all the fruit that her words would produce till the end of time. This surely included the benefits derived from her writings.

The recurrent celebration of the feast of the Purification brought many signs of the benevolence of the Blessed Virgin toward the community at Helfta. Once when the nuns were chanting *"Ora pro populo"* on this feast, she knelt between the community and her divine Son, interceding for each sister individually. Then, having seated herself near him on the throne of glory, she commanded the choir of angels to join their shields around the convent and defend it against the enemy of souls.

The singing of the *Salve* at Compline on the feast of the Assumption was marked by a revelation of Our Lady's protection. At the words, "Turn then thine eyes of mercy toward us," she directed the eyes of Christ toward the earth, saying, "These are my merciful eyes; I turn them on all who invoke me, and they shall thence obtain the fruit of eternal salvation."

It was on this feast also that Gertrude saw sinners under the forms of various animals running to conceal themselves under Mary's mantle. She sheltered them with great kindness and stroked them affectionately "as one strokes a little dog." St. Alphonsus Liguori cites this episode in his treatise, *The Glories of Mary.*

Our Lady showed great joy when Gertrude saluted her with the words, *"Ecce ancilla Domini,"* on the feast of the Annunciation, commemorating the delight that filled the heart of Mary when she abandoned herself to the will of God at the time of the Incarnation. "When anyone recalls that joy to me," said Our Lady, "I shall show myself a mother, as the words of the hymn request: *'Monstra te esse matrem.'* I shall appear to him as truly the mother of the King and supreme Pontiff."

In a vision to St. Gertrude, a vivid illustration of the charity of Our Lady took the form of a beautiful garden of flowers in which she stood. The blossoms farthest from her were more brilliant and fragrant than those close to her. As St. Gertrude wondered at this, she was told that it signified the greater merit won by actions prompted by extensive charity. This is an example of the doctrinal soundness of St. Gertrude's writings.

PERSONAL DEVOTIONS

Many biblical texts served to express Gertrude's love for the feast of the nativity. Once, following the verse from the *Song of Songs,* "A bundle of myrrh is my beloved to me," she gathered together all the sufferings of the Divine Infant under the image of this pungent herb. Like St. Bernard, who had made the same association, Gertrude meditated with compassionate love and gratitude on the weakness and discomforts of the Christchild.

On one occasion at mass, as she endeavored to form in her heart a stable for the Infant, she saw all the good works which men had accomplished by God's help adorning the walls of the stable like little bells. One vision of the Infant Jesus anticipates Dali's painting, "the Virgin of Port Lligat." In it, Gertrude saw the Child in his mother's womb, which was transparent as pure crystal, and she understood that as his humanity was nourished by her virginal milk, so his divinity was served by her love and purity. At the end of mass, our Lady, clothed in the double glory of virginity and motherhood, came forth and embracing each sister, presented her Child to each. Some received him carefully, taking pains that he might suffer no discomfort, but others, whose wills were stubborn and inflexible, held him in an awkward position.

THE PASSION

It has been said that the spirituality of the Middle Ages was marked by "the passion for the Passion of Christ." Gertrude's devotion to the sufferings and death of the

Savior is revealed in many of her writings. Indeed, one of her lost works is a poem on the Passion.

Since devotion to the Passion is always associated with the wish to make atonement for the sins of the world, the contemporary biographer of St. Gertrude says that Christ, responding to this desire, sought to find repose in the heart of the saint when he was offended by the crimes of mankind. (A similar honor was given to St. Mechtild and to St. Catherine de Ricci to whom Christ said: "I desire to take refuge in your heart and in the hearts of my other daughters.")

Gertrude was ingenious in devising various means of offering reparation to Christ for the pains and insults he had endured; many of these devotions she taught to others. (She once accused herself of neglecting to perform what she had instructed others to do.) In all her exercises in honor of the Passion Gertrude was mindful of the homage offered by the entire Church; she also said special prayers for the Church at these times. She was accustomed to venerate the holy wounds individually, each for a special intention—for example, the right hand for omission of good words and works. Then as she adored the wound in the side of Christ, she begged him to supply to the Church whatever was wanting to her perfections and merits.

While generously performing work beyond her strength, she remembered what Christ suffered when his hands and feet were painfully stretched on the cross. Similarly, she practiced devotions in honor of his agonizing anticipation of his Passion on Holy Thursday, his words on the cross, his crown of thorns, and his death. In all these exercises she never lost sight of the needs of others, sinners in particular.

It was revealed to Gertrude that although the sins of the laity are like thorns which tear the divine face of Christ, those of religious are knotted whips causing more secret but far more bitter suffering.

THE HOLY FACE OF CHRIST

St. Gertrude had a great love of the Holy Face of Christ, bruised and disfigured during the Passion. Many of her prayers call upon Christ to show his face to his servants. "Alas," she writes, "how much longer is my soul to be debarred from the presence of thy longed-for countenance?" One of St. Gertrude's mystical experiences was an intellectual vision of the Holy Face through which Christ gave her a transcendent illumination and participation in his divinity. Her *Exercises* contain many allusions to this favor; in the sixth *Exercise* she exclaims, "O my God . . . the light of whose glorious face hath set its mark upon me despite my unworthiness." Once when she asked, "O Lord, how can we soothe the anguish of your gentle face?" he answered, "Anyone who meditates lovingly upon my Passion and prays for sinners prepares an excellent remedy."

THE CRUCIFIX

The sight of a crucifix always moved Gertrude profoundly. She considered that every loving thought and glance directed toward it was reciprocated by the merciful gaze of Christ, saying: "See how for your love I have been fastened to the cross, naked and scorned, after enduring a severe scourging and the dislocation of my members. My heart is so seized by love that if it were necessary for your salvation, I should desire to undergo for you alone the unspeakable pangs that I suffered for the whole world."

One of Gertrude's most memorable sayings is that no one ever looks at a crucifix except by the special providence of God, nor does a person ever look at one devoutly without receiving some great benefit. Once as she was venerating the crucifix, she understood that we should hide all our sufferings whether of mind or body in the sufferings of Christ "as we place a prop in a bundle of faggots."

MARKS OF GERTRUDE'S SPIRITUALITY

Once when someone asked Christ what most pleased him in St. Gertrude, he answered, "Her liberty of spirit." The spiritual freedom that prevailed in the medieval cloister contrasts sharply with the atmosphere in some convents during later centuries, the seventeenth in particular. Without fear of novelty, the men and women of the Middle Ages expressed their devotion in imaginative, even naive ways. Gertrude once replaced the nails in her crucifix with sweet-smelling cloves; Blessed Henry Suso crowned the statue of our Lady with roses; St. Francis of Assisi would sometimes take up a piece of wood from the ground and draw another stick across it as if playing a viol, "then suiting his movements to the rhythm, he would sing of our Lord Jesus in the language of France." These innovations were not, of course, introduced into the communal exercises. They were an expression of youth and intense vitality, the energetic fervor of individuals at a time when, as Canon John Gay puts it, "all living people were young."

St. Gertrude's forthright expression of her liberty of spirit may be paralleled in the words of other medieval women mystics. St. Catherine of Siena said to Christ, "I wish you to have everything and your enemy nothing." Mezzi Sibriwin, a Dominican nun at Töss, anticipated the famous epitaph of Martin Elginbrodde when she exclaimed, "My Lord, if you were Mezzi Sibriwin and I were God, I should wish that you were God and I were Mezzi." —In our own day, St. Thérèse of Lisieux's last written words echo this declaration, but with reference to the Blessed Mother.[6]

These are more or less superficial manifestations of a liberty of spirit which, Vernet asserts, is found only in the highest forms of the mystical state. When the moment of intense union has passed—*rara hora, parva mora,* writes Bernard, and Gertrude echoes him—the person re-enters the common life, walking by the light of faith, often uncertain, doubtful, even tormented by human weaknesses and needing the counsel of others. Nevertheless, the intercourse with divinity has left the spirit reinforced, given it a new principle of action, greater detachment and self-renunciation—all of which constitute liberty of spirit in a larger sense.

ENERGY

Allied to this freedom of spirit is vigor or energy—a trait which we may call "classic" in great women saints. It is what we admire in the valiant woman of the Book of Proverbs, in the mother of the Macchabees, in Judith, among the women of the Old Testament. In the New Dispensation it is found even in the child St. Agnes, in St. Agatha, St. Catherine of Alexandria, St. Joan of Arc, St. Catherine of Siena, St. Teresa of Avila. *"Fecisti viriliter,"* the Church sings to them; "thou hast done manfully." So too St. Gertrude, in her fifth *Exercise* prays, "Gird my thigh with the sword of thy Spirit, O thou most mighty, and give me a manly heart that I may strive after the virtues manfully and resolutely." Fearless in matters concerning God's honor or the salvation of souls, she acted and spoke uncompromisingly.

Yet this vigor was never directed to her own defense.

[6] In its original form, this sentiment has been attributed to St. Augustine, but the attribution has been questioned.

The mysterious sentence of her contemporary biographer, never explained, remains to testify that Gertrude had enemies whom she did not resist; "She sought only the glory of God rather than her own; she not only sought it, she pursued it with ardor to the point of sacrificing to it her honor, her life, and in a certain sense, her soul." With this testimony we may associate Gertrude's own declaration: "Although after my death I should undergo the torments of hell for my folly, nevertheless I should rejoice if through my labors the Lord God might receive honor from others."

As Père Léonard has said: "The consciousness of the abyss which separates the uncreated Being from the creature, the still more immeasurable distance which divides the sinner from absolute Holiness, characterize Christian mysticism. The necessity of grace, of a benevolent inclination on God's part, before the abyss can be bridged, springs inevitably from this."[7]

One such bridging of the abyss through the communication of the merits of Christ is represented by an experience of Gertrude's on an Easter Monday, perhaps the anniversary of her reception of the habit. She had asked Christ to supply by the merits of the Eucharist for all her negligences in obeying the rule. It then seemed to her that the Savior presented her to his Father. She was wearing her habit, which was made of as many pieces as she had spent years in the order. In each year she could distinguish all her thoughts, words, and actions, good and bad; moreover, the motive of each was apparent. Among her imperfections was an occasional use of diplomacy to secure her own way. When, however, the Son of God had offered for her to his Father all the merits of his holy life, the tunic appeared to be covered with brilliant plates of gold.

[7] A. Léonard, pp. 111-112.

CONFIDENCE

The confidence inspired by such revelations of God's mercy was the basis of the holy familiarity of Gertrude's intercourse with Christ. Her inquiries into the divine purpose in leaving some evils unremedied, her respectful demands as to why some petitions are unanswered, her gentle insistence that her dying sisters be consoled in their last moments, all show the confidence of a daughter at ease with a generous father. Yet she is invariably reverent. As to St. Teresa of Avila so to her, God is king or emperor, the divine majesty.

With both Gertrude and Teresa the confidence might sometimes approach playfulness.[8]

Although Gertrude's humor was evidently less robust, she enjoyed recreations, having been assured by Christ that he finds delight in the hearts of his joyful servants just as a father takes pleasure in a minstrel who is entertaining the family. Frequently it is recorded "Smiling *(subridens)* Christ answered her."

The saint's joyful confidence was reinforced when the Lord told her that the poems she composed in his honor gave him as much delight "as a person whose friend leads him through a garden filled with music and the fragrance of flowers and fruits." Moreover, he told her, not the least movement of her finger, not even a single thought for his love should go unrewarded. (This recalls the saying of Jean Cocteau: "If God numbers the hairs of our head, does he not also count the syllables of our poems?")

[8] Remember the mock-solemn hymn wherein the Spanish saint invoked God to banish vermin from the garments of the community: "Free this serge from denizens so threatening! *(Librad de la mala gente este sayal)*"

172

LOVE AND GRATITUDE

However varied the saint's expressions of her devotion, their source was the consuming love of God. Ancelet-Hustache has well said, "Charity constitutes sanctity and charity is in the will, not in visions or illuminations however sublime." The alternate acknowledgement of God's transcendence and her own incapacity to love and honor him worthily are the systole and diastole of Gertrude's spiritual life. She echoes the cry of St. Bernard in his *De Diligendo Deo:* "My God, my help, I love you as much as I can—not as much as I ought, but at least as much as I can."

Christ's response to the love he inspired in his "spear-maiden" is not within our competence to describe. That Gertrude was favored with the stigmata, that she received the wound of love, that the Lord disclosed and imparted to her his Sacred Heart—these are the recorded episodes out of many that the saint herself could not reveal. The compilers of the *Legatus,* who knew her well, likewise confess their inability to do so. Yet all is summed up in the words of Christ, the text inscribed on some of the portraits of St. Gertrude: "After the sacrament of the altar, you will find me in the heart of Gertrude." The fine baroque statue of the saint in the Benedictine church at Zwiefalten, Germany, shows her open heart enclosing a small figure of the Christchild.

St. Gertrude's gratitude for the gifts of God breaks forth in almost every line of Book Two of the *Legatus.* A touching proof of her appreciation of her great graces is her loving recollection not only of the days, but often of the very hours when she received these favors.

Gertrude's love of God involved the love of her neighbor, especially the members of her community. She was on terms of great intimacy with more than one of the nuns.

173

Knowledge of many of her graces comes to us through the reports of those with whom she was intimate; it seems that they came to realize her privileges through supernatural revelation and against her will. "I had not disclosed these things to anyone," she writes, "yet I heard from their lips the secrets of my heart."

Gertrude's complete abandonment to God's pleasure must have been evident to those who consulted her. Christ had said to her: "If you wish me to find complete delight in your heart, permit me to do with it whatever I wish, without caring whether I give you consolation or bitterness." Again she was taught, "Your will is the key to your heart. Give it to me."

"Gertrude was truly the spouse of Christ," says Pourrat. "Transformed in him, she had no other desire than to accomplish his holy will in all things." Vernet ranks her with Angela of Foligno and Catherine of Siena as "a star of the first magnitude." Among the canonized saints who have admired and cited her teachings are Alphonsus Liguori, Francis de Sales, and Thérèse of Lisieux. When we add to these the approbation of the Venerable Louis Blosius, Cornelius a Lapide, Francisco Ribera, confessor and biographer of St. Teresa, M. Olier, Dom Alban Butler, and Mother Cornelia Connelly, it is clear that she attracts more than one type of spiritual personality. In our own day, Ernest Hello, Juan Arintero, Dom Columba Marmion, and Reginald Garrigou-Lagrange have quoted her teachings in their works. Cardinal Merry del Val always kept with him the little volume of St. Gertrude's prayers with his own marginal notations.

In her simplicity of intention and purity of affection, St. Gertrude is in the timeless company of those who have chosen Christ in preference to all others. A passage in the *Mystical Vine* speaks for all of them, addressing the men and women of every generation. Every phrase of this passage could be illustrated by an episode from the life of St. Gertrude:

"What do you seek that you will not find in him? The Lord Jesus Christ is all that you can desire. If you are ill, he is your physician. If you are fighting, he is your defender. If you are thirsty, he is drink; if cold, he is your garment. If you are sad, he is joy. If you are in darkness, he is light. If you are orphaned, he is Father. He is Spouse, he is Friend, he is Brother. He is most high, most good, most merciful, most strong, most comely, most wise, who endlessly rules all things. But what need of so many words? Whatever you desire, you have in Jesus Christ."

Saint of the Sacred Heart

Long before the marauding Prince-Bishop, Albert of Halberstadt, had set fire to Helfta some forty years after St. Gertrude's death, a more enduring flame had been lit within the convent walls. Even today, centuries after the assault on the monastery and the removal of the nuns, the memory of the convent at Helfta is a sanctuary lamp burning among ruins. Here where the Sacred Heart of Jesus was exalted, the names of St. Gertrude and St. Mechtild are forever linked to the devotion which illuminated their monastery, for it was chiefly through their ardor that Helfta became a shrine of adoration, love, and reparation. Not only these two saints, but also the Abbess Gertrude and Mechtild the ex-beguine of Magdeburg—in fact the entire community—are to some extent associated with the veneration of the Sacred Heart. It may even be maintained that Helfta provides the first instance of communal acceptance of the cult, since St. Gertrude, its chief advocate, did not meet the type of opposition that was to assail St. Margaret Mary four centuries later.

HISTORY OF THE DEVOTION

Devotion to the Sacred Heart, based on the fact of the Incarnation, is rooted in Scripture, Christian tradition, and liturgy. The theology of the first Christian millennium makes repeated mention of the fountain of living water

176

from the wound in the side of Christ. In the torrent of sacramental grace the Latin fathers saw a fulfillment of the prophecy of Isaias (XII, 3): "You shall draw waters with joy from the fountain of the Savior." The birth of the Church *"ex aqua et sanguine"* from the wounded side of the new Adam asleep in death was, they affirmed, a parallel to the birth of Eve from the side of the sleeping Adam. "Both dogmatically and historically, this vision of the Church proceeding from the Heart of our Lord was a fundamental notion of the early Christians."[1]

The image of the wound in the side of Christ as an inexhaustible fountain of redemptive life through the Church and the sacraments sums up the history of patristic thought on this subject. It is an objective attitude which looks back to the time of the crucifixion. Although in the Middle Ages it was supplemented by another concept, it was not supplanted, and this objective element remained basic to the theology and liturgy of the Sacred Heart, as indeed it still does.

Concomitant with the idea of the wound in Christ's side as a fountain of life arose a particular veneration for the apostle John who, St. Augustine says, "received from the Lord on whose breast he lay at the Last Supper (in order to signify that he drew loftier mysteries from his inmost Heart) a special and peculiar gift,"... namely, the ability to communicate the spirit of the Son of God. So too, Paulinus writes: "John, who rested blissfully on the breast of our Lord was inebriated with the Holy Spirit; from the Heart of the all-creating Wisdom he quaffed an understanding that transcends any creature's."[2]

[1] Hugo Rahner, "The Beginnings of the Devotion in Patristic Times" in *Heart of the Savior:* A Symposium, ed. Josef Stierli (New York, 1958) p. 51.
[2] *Ibid.*

177

In the transition from the patristic to the Middle Ages, St. John is a key figure, serving to unite the earlier objective concept described above with an emerging deeply emotional and subjective veneration.

Meditation on the *Song of Songs* played a major part among the influences contributing to this fruitful synthesis. As early as the sixth century, Gregory the Great had applied the words, "Come, my dove in the clefts of the rocks, in the hollow places of the wall," to the wounded side of Christ as the refuge of the soul. By the eleventh century the number of such reflections is impressive. St. Anselm of Canterbury, meditating on the Passion of Christ, exclaimed: "What sweetness in his pierced side! That wound has given us a glimpse of the treasure house of his goodness, that is to say, of the love of his Heart for us." St. Bernard likewise spoke of the mystery of the Sacred Heart in these words: "The secret of his Heart lies visible through the clefts of his body; visible too the great mystery of his love."

The influence of St. Bernard's commentary on the *Song of Songs* gave also new warmth and impetus to the concept of the Heart of Christ as an immediate presence. Gilbert of Holland, who continued Bernard's unfinished treatise, found his greatest inspiration in the verse, "Thou hast wounded my heart, my sister, my spouse." In a passage which recalls the significance of St. Gertrude's name (dear lance) he writes: "Shall we not call that soul blessed which pierces with the darts of its love the vast Heart of our Lord Jesus Christ? . . . Weary not of wounding thy Beloved, O faithful spouse! Let thy acts of love be as darts to pierce him."

Others who paid similar tribute to the Divine Heart either implicitly or explicitly were the Saints Anthony of

Padua, Clare, Thomas Aquinas, Francis of Assisi, and Albert the Great.

Among all of St. Gertrude's predecessors in the love of the Sacred Heart, St. Lutgarde of Aywières, a Cistercian stigmatic of the early thirteenth century, is of special interest. To her was granted the first recorded vision of the Sacred Heart in the Middle Ages. At the age of fifteen, she had a revelation of the wounded Christ who showed her his pierced Heart. Until that time, although she had been living in a convent (perhaps only as a student) Lutgarde's life had been worldly, even frivolous. With the realization of God's love which accompanied this vision, she began to live for him only. Once when Christ asked her what she wished, she answered him: "I want your Heart." "And still more do I want yours," he told her. Thomas Merton has said that St. Lutgarde is perhaps the first saint of whom the mystical exchange of hearts is recorded. He explains that the term is purely symbolic: "There is no question of a physical exchange, but only of a mystical union of wills."[3]

In a subsequent conversation, Christ said to St. Lutgarde: "Do you not see how I offer myself entirely to the Father for my sinners? In the same way I would have you offer yourself entirely to me for my sinners." This request emphasized the privilege of reparation which is implicit in both the medieval and the modern devotion to the Sacred Heart.

SAINTS OF THE SACRED HEART

If one were to enumerate the saints of the Sacred Heart, the first place would, of course, be given to the Mother of

[3] Thomas Merton, *What Are These Wounds?* (Milwaukee, 1950) p. 15.

179

Christ, whose closeness to the Heart of her Son is unique.[4] Next would come St. John the beloved disciple.

His paramount role in the history of the objective devotion has already been noted. As the chosen friend and patron of St. Gertrude he appeared to her on a day in Advent, magnificently attired in a golden mantle and a breastplate inscribed: *In principio erat Verbum*. Again, on his own feast, pointing reverently to the bosom of Christ, he said to her: "Behold, this is the Holy of Holies, drawing to itself all that is good in heaven and earth." He then placed Gertrude near the wounded side of the Savior where she could hear the pulsations of the Sacred Heart. "Why is it, O beloved of God," she asked him, "that you who rested on his bosom at the Last Supper have said nothing of what you experienced then?" St. John answered: "It was my task to present to the first age of the Church the doctrine of the word made flesh, which no human intellect can ever fully comprehend. The eloquence of that sweet beating of his Heart is reserved for the last age in order that the world grown cold and torpid may be set on fire with the love of God."

The first sentence of St. John's reply recalls the patristic theology described earlier in this chapter. His next sentence conveys the subjective devotion which became dominant in the Middle Ages. This juxtaposition of the two aspects of the veneration of the Heart of Christ makes St. Gertrude's vision unique. As Jean Bainvel writes, "It forms an epoch in the history of the devotion to the Sacred Heart."[5]

Between St. John and St. Gertrude as saints of the

---

[4] "Devotion to the Heart of Jesus" *Catholic Encyclopedia* (New York, 1910) VII, 165.

[5] Abbé Louis Chasle, *Sister Mary of the Divine Heart* (London, 1911) xii.

Sacred Heart are grouped all those others, such as Anselm, Francis of Assisi and Bernard, whose meditations and mystical intuitions prepared the spiritual climate for the flowering of the devotion in St. Gertrude and St. Mechtild. It becomes evident that the saints of Helfta are not isolated from the spiritual currents of their times. Rather, the eminence of their convent, of their personalities, and of their graces makes them instrumental in emphasizing the warmly personal, immediate, and contemporary quality of their relations with the Sacred Heart. That devout lay persons today see the Sacred Heart as immediate and present is owing in no small measure to the influence of the saints of Helfta as well as to St. Margaret Mary.

The history of the devotion since Gertrude's time is of course still in progress. Certain major figures, however, should be mentioned here. In the seventeenth century, the three saints of the Sacred Heart—John Eudes, Claude de la Colombière, and Margaret Mary—illustrate the movement toward liturgical homage to the Heart of Christ. In 1670, St. John Eudes' book, *The Devotion to the Adorable Heart of Jesus,* preceded by three years the first revelation to St. Margaret Mary. Because he was the first to compose masses and offices in honor of the Sacred Hearts of Jesus and Mary, and also caused their feasts to be observed by the religious of his order, Leo XIII called St. John Eudes "Institutor of the Liturgical Cult of the Sacred Hearts of Jesus and Mary."

Mysteriously linked with St. Gertrude, another apostle of the Sacred Heart appears at the end of the nineteenth century, Mother Mary of the Divine Heart, a Sister of the Order of the Good Shepherd. Born Countess Droste zu Vischering in 1863 at Munster, she entered the Good Shepherd novitiate in 1888. Eventually she was made superior of a convent in Oporto, Portugal, where she died in

1890 on the vigil of the feast of the Sacred Heart. Cardinal Merry del Val, secretary of state to Pius X, has asserted, "It was, in fact, principally through the intervention of Mary Droste zu Vischering that the twentieth century opened under the happy auspices of the Sacred Heart."

Mother Mary was devoted to St. Teresa, St. Catherine of Siena, and St. Gertrude; her greatest attachment, however, was to the last-named, whom Christ had given her "as sister and companion." Moreover, many of her traits were similar to those of the saint of Helfta, who appeared to her several times in visions. Her biographer declares that in her act of consecration to the Sacred Heart, Mother Mary's eloquent simplicity shows her to be a true sister of St. Gertrude.

Mother Mary contributed to the honoring of the Sacred Heart by suggesting to Leo XIII the consecration of the entire human race; this he considered the greatest act of his pontificate. On one occasion, the pontiff told her parents, the Count and Countess Droste zu Vischering, that he had determined to perform this act "on account of the communication which your daughter made to me . . . tell her clearly that it is in consequence of what she made known to me that I have come to this decision."

If it is asked why the revelation made to St. Margaret Mary needed to be supplemented by the apostolate of Mother Mary of the Divine Heart, the following passage from her own account will give the answer: "Once, when speaking on this same subject of communion, he said that his desire had been to establish the cultus of his Divine Heart, and that as this external worship had now been introduced and spread on all sides by his apparition to Blessed Margaret Mary, he wished that the interior worship should also be more and more established. That is to say, Christ desired that souls should acquire a habit of uniting themselves more and more with him, offering their hearts to be his dwelling."

THE SACRED HEART AT HELFTA

At Helfta, according to Jeannette Ancelet-Hustache, it was the ex-beguine, Mechtild von Magdeburg, who originated devotion to the Sacred Heart. Like many mystics before her, Mechtild did indeed honor the wounds of Christ and often spoke ardently of his "heart's blood" as a sign of his love for man. The pierced Heart of Christ was for her the incarnation of his inner life.

In the first part of her work, *The Flowing Light of the Godhead,* a chapter entitled "Of the Presence at Court of the Soul to Whom God Shows Himself," contains the following lines: "He with great desire shows her his Divine Heart. It glows like red gold in a great fire. And God lays the soul in his glowing Heart so that he, the great God, and she, the humble maid, embrace and are one as water with wine." In the same book Mechtild also represents Christ as saying, "How fiery my Heart!" and again, "Thy heart's desire shalt thou lay nowhere but in mine own Divine Heart." Such passages, however, are rare and not representative of the general tone of Mechtild von Magdeburg's writing.

A more characteristic sentence may be quoted from one of her prayers: "Together with all your creatures, I long here and now for your glory in all things and through all things, as they flowed spotless from your loving Heart."

A comparison of her work with that of her companions, St. Gertrude and St. Mechtild, shows that as Dom Pierre Doyère observes, her "spiritual orientation" is somewhat different. The dominant image in her book is expressed in its title, *The Flowing Light of the Godhead.*

As her admirers rightly assert, Mechtild von Magdeburg

is "a true Minnesinger of the Holy Spirit," "an exquisite poet and visionary." If it is inaccurate to say that she is the originator of the devotion to the Sacred Heart at Helfta, she is nevertheless a sharer in this devotion and certainly one of the luminaries of medieval German mysticism.

THE ABBESS GERTRUDE AND THE SACRED HEART

There is no evidence that the Abbess Gertrude von Hackeborn shared revelations of the Sacred Heart, nor indeed that she was favored with any extraordinary graces. Nevertheless, her recognition of the special favors accorded to St. Gertrude and to St. Mechtild must have won for her a notable recompense. After her death she appeared to St. Gertrude and said: "For you, my daughter, I have received a special reward from God because I have urged you on with faithful affection in the affair you know of, for the greater glory of God. . . . All the heavenly court pays me homage on this account." One may reasonably conjecture from this remark that the abbess had encouraged and even urged St. Gertrude to write the account of her spiritual life.

In St. Mechtild's *Book of Special Grace,* it is recorded that when her sister the Abbess Gertrude was dying, Mechtild saw her enter into the Sacred Heart as into an open sanctuary. Later, when the bereaved community sang the line, "You who repose in the shadow of the Beloved," (from the responsory, *Surge Virgo*) the voice of the dead abbess answered: "It would not be enough for me to be in his shadow; it is in the Heart of the Well-Beloved that I rest in sweetness, serenity, and peace." Soon after this, when Mechtild prayed to her sister to intercede for all the nuns, the abbess said to her: "I urge my daughters to obtain for themselves the sweet repose where I now

live with such security, in the most sweet Heart of Jesus."
It was St. Mechtild also who saw a great concourse of the
members of the congregation gathering in a festival dance
around the abbess on the anniversary of her death. Their
song, *"O Mater Nostra,"* entered into the Heart of Christ
from which it emerged as a simple melody of marvelous
beauty, seeming like an anticipation of Dante's description
of the song of the just in the *Divine Comedy.*

ST. MECHTILD AND THE SACRED HEART

Although the prophecy of the future triumph of the
Sacred Heart was made not to St. Mechtild but to St. Gertrude, her life too was permeated by this devotion. Gertrude herself testified after her friend's death: "This angelic
maiden is most fittingly compared to the seraphim, for she
was so directly united to God who is love itself, so ardently
attached to his flaming heart that she was made one spirit
with him."

To Mechtild, even more often than to Gertrude, the
Sacred Heart was revealed as a magnificent dwelling, the
House of Gold. Within the mansion she saw four beautiful maidens—Humility, Patience, Sweetness, and Charity.
At another time, entering the same mansion, Mechtild perceived a great cross engraved on the pavement. As she
prostrated herself upon it, a golden dart from the center of
the cross pierced her to the soul. (The Solesmes editors
relate this to the similar transverberations of St. Gertrude
and St. Teresa of Avila, as indicating a relationship in
their states of perfection.)

In her painful illnesses, St. Mechtild was accustomed
to take refuge in the Heart of Christ as in a house of repose.
She learned also that one may knock three times at the
Sacred Heart as the Gate of Heaven by praising the power

of the Father, the wisdom of the Son, and the goodness of the Holy Spirit.

One image of the Sacred Heart is unique in its informality. After receiving a great grace—which she does not specify—St. Mechtild, overcome by a sense of her unworthiness, exclaimed: "O generous King! So magnificent a gift is not suitable for me. I am not worthy to serve in your kitchen and to wash the vessels there." The Saviour asked her kindly: "And what is my kitchen and what are the vessels you wish to cleanse there?" Mechtild was silent, not knowing what to say. But Christ answered the question himself: "The kitchen is my divine Heart. As the kitchen is a place open to all, to slaves as well as to free men, so my Heart is always open to all, and ready to give everyone what he desires. The ruler in the kitchen is the Holy Spirit whose inexpressible kindness fills my Heart with overflowing generosity. My vessels are the hearts of my saints and my chosen ones who continually partake of the ravishing abundance of my divine Heart."

Once after communion, Christ said to Mechtild: "Thou in me and I in thee. Be submerged in my omnipotence like the fish in the ocean." "O Lord," she answered, "fish are often caught in the net. What if that should happen to me?" The Savior replied: "You cannot be drawn forth from me. You will make your nest in my divine Heart. . . . The nest is sincere humility, maintained among all the gifts and favors I have imparted to you."

The prayers of St. Mechtild give constant evidence of her devotion to the Sacred Heart. Among the numerous invocations, a few may be noted. Obeying the instruction of Christ, she greeted him each morning with the salutation: "Praise, benediction, glory, and salvation to the most sweet and benevolent Heart of Jesus Christ, my most true lover. I thank you for the faithful watch with which you have surrounded me during this night in which you have unceasingly offered to God the Father the thanksgiving and homage that I owe him. And now I offer you my heart as a fresh rose that its fragrance may delight your divine Heart." When any suffering came to her, she would say, "O love, the bearer of these pains to me from the Heart of God, I offer this to thee. I pray that with all my gratitude thou wilt return them to me made perfect." She also advised others to make this offering.

On one occasion the Blessed Virgin led St. Mechtild to venerate the wounds of her Son, saying to her: "Come and greet the wound in the dear Heart of my Son, for it is that Heart that feels the suffering of all the wounds of his body."

Another time, in a letter to a friend, Mechtild wrote: "God makes a gift of his divine Heart to the soul in order that it may give him its heart in return. One ought carefully to keep the Heart of God and consider well what most pleases him."

In their writings, both St. Mechtild and St. Gertrude frequently describe the Sacred Heart as sending forth streams of light, or rivers of crystal clarity. In addition, St. Mechtild represents the Heart as producing three fragrant streams of allegorical significance: the first stream has the perfume of rosewater, to manifest the love distilled in the furnace of charity from "that most noble rose" the Sacred Heart; the second has the fragrance of rich wine from the royal blood shed on the winepress of the cross; the third odor is sweet balm from the divine Heart which death itself cannot change to bitterness. In the odor of these three ointments the soul runs in love and desire, according to the words of the *Song of Songs:* "Draw me after thee; we will run in the odor of thy ointments."

Like St. Gertrude, Mechtild was privileged to listen

to the pulsations of the Sacred Heart. Embracing the Christchild, she marveled at the strange beating of his infant Heart—a strong triple pulsation followed by a lighter one. He explained to her: "My Heart did not beat like that of other men; from my infancy to my death the pulsations were as you hear. That is why I died so quickly on the cross." The infinite impetuosity of his love in its various manifestations accounted for the three vehement pulsations; the fourth represented his mildness and gentleness toward men in giving them an example that they could imitate. At another time, St. Mechtild heard in the vigorous beating of the divine Heart a repeated invitation: "Come and repent, come and be reconciled, come and be consoled, come and be blessed. Come, my sister, to possess the eternal inheritance that I obtained for you by my blood. Come, my spouse, to rejoice in my divinity."

Again, after communion, the three pulsations of the Heart of Christ were interpreted as three words addressed to her: "*Come:* that is to say, separate yourself from all creatures; *Enter,* with confidence, as a spouse; *Into the bridal chamber,* that is the divine Heart."

On more than one occasion, as he had done to St. Gertrude, Christ gave his Heart to St. Mechtild as a pledge of his love. This is recorded as one of the first graces she received. During Easter week as she intoned the Mass, *Venite, Benedicti,* she felt a sudden extraordinary joy. Turning to the Savior, she prayed, "Oh, if only I could be one of the blessed ones to hear that sweet word!" "Be assured of that," he answered. "I shall give you my Heart as a pledge of it. You will have it with you always and on the day when your desire is to be granted, you will restore it to me in testimony. I give you my Heart also to be your refuge so that at the hour of death, no other road will open to you but that of my Heart where you will rest forever."

The ring of betrothal is also associated with Mechtild's entering into the Heart of Christ as through a portal. In the long passage quoted in a preceding chapter, wherein Christ relates the stages of his passion to the parts of a dance, he concludes: "After this I opened my Heart for thee to enter in."

During the last days of St. Mechtild von Hackeborn it seemed that after her anointing she lived in an aura of spiritual light sent forth from the Sacred Heart. In response to her act of love, the Savior poured out a torrent of graces upon the whole Church, and especially upon all who were present at her deathbed. At the moment of her departure from life on the feast of St. Elizabeth (November 19) he reminded her of the gift of his Heart which he had made to her several years before, and asked her gently, "Where is my pledge?" At these words, the saint offered her own heart to him and breathed her last as he received it. After Mechtild's death, St. Gertrude realized that her holy friend obtained all manner of graces from the Sacred Heart for those who invoked her. It appeared also that her beatitude was drawn from the same Heart that she had so honored in life and death.

It would seem that the intense love for their community felt by both St. Gertrude and St. Mechtild drew down upon all the sisters the blessing of the Sacred Heart, especially at the hour of death. One sister revealed after her death that although she was rewarded by possession of the treasure of the Heart of Jesus, yet one of its gifts was withheld from her because she had not sufficiently shared the graces she had received, when to manifest them would have contributed to the glory of God.

Another death reported by St. Gertrude in her *Legatus*

189

is that of "Sister M." whom the Solesmes editors conjecture to be the other Mechtild, the ex-beguine of Magdeburg. According to Gertrude's account, the breath of the dying nun appeared in the form of a golden vapor which flowed toward the Sacred Heart. (This is a curious and touching reversal of the image conveyed by the title of Mechtild's book, *Lux Fluens Divinitatis*.)

ST. GERTRUDE AND THE SACRED HEART

One of St. Gertrude's first references to the Heart of Christ occurs seven years after the account of her conversion. She had asked someone, perhaps St. Mechtild, sister of the Abbess Gertrude, to say the following prayer for her every day before a crucifix: "O Lord, by thy pierced Heart, pierce her heart with the arrow of thy love so that nothing earthly may remain therein, but that it may be entirely filled with the virtue of thy divinity."

Soon afterward, Gertrude herself implored this favor at the moment when she was receiving communion: "Lord, I confess that by my own merits I am not worthy to receive the least of thy graces; but by the merits and desires of all here present, I beseech thee to pierce my heart with the arrow of thy love." It was in answer to this prayer that the saint received one of her greatest privileges, the deep, desired, and incurable wound of divine love, when a ray of light came from the wound of the right side in the image of the crucified Savior. Mechtild's prayer for Gertrude associates this event with the Sacred Heart, whereas the account previously quoted (page 81) does not do so.

It was, St. Gertrude writes, by the advice of a certain person that she sought to honor with faithful devotion the love of the pierced Heart of Jesus; to draw from that fountain of charity the water to wash away all her offenses; to find in it the oil of gratitude as an unfailing remedy for

190

all sorrow; and to obtain there the bond of justification whereby all her thoughts, words, and works would be united inseparably to him. One surmises that this enlightened confidant was St. Mechtild, for Gertrude says that these things were disclosed to her "by a person who as I hope had accustomed herself to listen to the gentle murmur of your loving voice with more delicacy and attention than (alas) I." The cadence of the Latin is particularly beautiful here: *"quae, ut spero, ad laudem tuam mentales aures suas multo stabilius magisque tenue assuefecit venis amatorii susurri tui, quam heu! ego."*

"BURNING FURNACE OF CHARITY"

In his manifestations to St. Gertrude, as later to St. Margaret Mary, Christ opened his Heart as a treasury from which all might draw infinite riches. In the Litany of the Sacred Heart, the invocation, "Burning furnace of charity" reminds one of the frequent references to divine love as described by St. Gertrude. Her account of the Sacred Heart penetrated by a consuming heat of love anticipates not only the revelation to St. Margaret Mary but the poem, "The Burning Babe," by the Elizabethan martyr, Robert Southwell, who wrote: "My faultless breast the furnace is." The invocation, "King and Center of all hearts," recalls St. Gertrude's numerous references to Christ as King and Emperor. If one remembers that the word which is translated "abode" in the invocation, "Abode of justice and love," is *receptaculum,* St. Gertrude's many images of the Sacred Heart as a vessel will come to mind. Finally, the invocation, "Hope of those who die in thee," might be taken as the title for the account of the many holy deaths at Helfta, not only St. Gertrude's and St. Mechtild's, but the Abbess Gertrude's, Mechtild of Magdeburg's and others.

191

In her seventh *Exercise,* "An Atonement for Sin and Preparation for Death," St. Gertrude calls upon the Sacred Heart in a series of moving and ardent exclamations: "O Heart, fountain of sweetness! O Heart surging with compassion! O Heart overflowing with charity! . . . O dearest Heart, I pray thee, engulf my whole heart in thee! . . . Come, and at the hour of my death open to me without delay the door of thy most benign Heart; my Beloved, by the pure intention of thy most holy thoughts and the ardent love of thy transpierced Heart, wash away all the guilt of my evil thought and of my sinful heart, that thy most bitter passion may be my shady bower in death, and thy Heart, broken by love, my everlasting dwelling-place, because thou alone art he whom I have chosen rather than all created things."

REVELATIONS OF THE SACRED HEART

Once on the vigil of Christmas Gertrude saw a light issuing from the Sacred Heart and forming a path whereby all might approach him. On another occasion, when she had been left alone in her illness "because the other sisters were engaged in their occupations," the Savior, "who never abandons those who are deprived of human consolation," showed her the wound in his side from which sprang forth as from his inmost Heart a pure stream, solid as crystal, forming on his breast a precious ornament alternating in color between gold and purple. He said to her: "This illness has so sanctified you that whenever you seem to go forth from me to the service of your neighbor by word, thought, or deed, you will be no more separated from me than this stream is separated from my Heart. As the gold and purple shine together with the crystal, so the cooperation of my divinity, symbolized by the gold and the perfect patience of my humanity symbolized by the purple, will make all your actions pleasing to me." Again, when Gertrude had ceased to write, fearing to give scandal by manifesting God's dealings with her, and felt unable to proceed even after his rebuke and a new grace of inspiration, she heard him say: "I shall draw you to my Heart and give you little by little all that you need. I shall act sweetly and gently, according to the measure of your strength."

Once when St. Gertrude implored God's assistance to overcome thoughts which distracted her in her preparation for communion, he said to her: "If anyone in temptation takes refuge with me, I can say of him: 'One is my dove, chosen among thousands; with one glance he has pierced my divine Heart. . . . The glance of my beloved which pierces my Heart is her confidence, tranquil and assured, that I can and will help her faithfully in everything.'" As she prayed for a person recommended to her, she saw a stream from the Sacred Heart, pure as crystal, flowing into the person. Similarly, she saw a golden channel extending from the Sacred Heart through which the virtue and beauty of the divine perfections poured into herself. During the rapture which followed this vision, the saint was mysteriously drawn into the Sacred Heart. Having chosen it for her temple, she was reminded by Christ of the example of St. Dominic: "Have you not read of some of my saints, such as my servant Dominic, who did not leave my temple but even ate and slept there?" The life of St. Dominic by Blessed Jordan of Saxony contains a reference to his sleeping in churches when exhausted by his vigils.

Gertrude perceived also that those persons who were perfectly submissive to the will of God drew many graces directly from the Sacred Heart of Christ, whereas those who tried to acquire virtue by following their natural inclinations and their own will, appeared to draw graces from his hands.

Another time, when the saint was importunately pleading to be released from earthly life, she was shown how God's mercy to sinners fills heaven with a concert of praise, giving pleasure to the Sacred Heart. Seeing then how many graces he pours forth on men during their mortal lives, she no longer desired to leave the flesh whereby he is so glorified.

St. Gertrude drew from the Sacred Heart all that she needed, even physical strength. When, for instance, she had passed an entire night without sleeping, she said: "By the tranquility with which you reposed for endless ages in the bosom of the Father; by the nine months in the womb of the Virgin Mary; by the joys that you experience in dwelling with a loving soul; I beseech you, O merciful God, to grant me a little rest, not for my own satisfaction, but for your eternal praise so that my exhausted strength may be restored."

In answer to her prayer, she was invited to rest on the Sacred Heart and received this instruction: "Anyone who is worn out by long wakefulness should say this prayer that you have just offered in order to regain the strength to sing my praises. If I do not grant the prayer and he endures his weariness with patience and humility, my divine kindness will receive him with much joy. A friend appreciates the love of one who deprives himself of sleep for the pleasure of conversing with him. His pleasure is the greater if his friend is ordinarily unable to sleep, yet rises gladly to talk with him. So too one who patiently offers me his infirmities, although sickness and insomnia have exhausted his strength, pleases me more than another whom perfect health allows to spend the entire night in prayer without any fatigue."

Once when Gertrude was grieving over the behavior of one of her friends who had repaid her kindness with contempt, Christ consoled her by offering her his Sacred Heart and saying: "Consider, my well beloved, the hidden secrets of my Heart. See how faithfully I have placed there all that you have done to please me and how I have enhanced it for the greater profit of your soul. See now whether you can ever reproach me for unfaithfulness even in a single word." As if to recompense her for her friend's ingratitude, Christ united her heart to his own, saying: "Henceforth your heart shall be a channel which from the abundant fountain of my Sacred Heart will pour forth torrents of divine consolation on those who dispose themselves to receive these outpourings by having recourse to you with confidence and humility."

When the saint was praying for someone who had sought her intercession, she received this instruction from Christ: "Let her make her nest in the crevice of the rock, that is to say, in the Sacred Heart, that she may rest in the depths of that cavern and taste the honey of the rock, that is, the aspirations of the Divine Heart. (These images are clearly a development of those in the meditations of St. Gregory and St. Anselm which were quoted earlier in this chapter.)

On one occasion Gertrude saw the consolations of the Holy Spirit under the figure of a stream of honey flowing from the Sacred Heart; at another time she was surprised to see a bitter current issuing. As she asked the meaning of this, Christ told her: "When someone gives money to his friend, the one who receives it is free to buy whatever he wishes. If he can buy either sweet or sour apples for the same price, he may prefer to buy the sour ones because they will keep better.

"Likewise when I consent to the prayers of my chosen

ones, I send the grace which will be of most benefit. For example, it is better for some persons to have trials rather than consolations in this life; and therefore when I pour out my grace upon them, they have more bitter sorrows and tribulations, by which they will receive ever more graces according to the pleasure of my divine Heart. The consolation that is stored up for them is hidden from them at present that they may labor the more faithfully, bearing their adversities patiently for the love of my name."

As the saint offered her own heart to Christ, she saw it united to his under the form of a chalice. "Grant, O loving God," she prayed, "that my heart may be always before you like those flasks that servants carry to refresh their masters; that you may have it filled or emptied when and for whom you wish." Pleased with this prayer, Christ turned to his Father, saying, "O holy Father, for your eternal praise may the heart of this creature pour forth over the world the inexhaustible stream of the benefits enclosed in my Sacred Heart."

Thereafter, whenever the saint offered her heart to God, it was so filled with thanks and praise that it appeared to add to the joy of the saints in heaven and to the advancement of the just on earth. This experience made Gertrude realize that it was God's pleasure for her to write in order that many might be helped.

A CONTRACT SEALED

In most paintings of St. Gertrude she is shown wearing seven rings on her right hand. This detail commemorates an episode told in her *Legatus*. One day as she was thinking of all that Christ had done for her, "I was so presumptuous," she says, "as to reproach him with not having sealed his promise by putting his hand in mine as is customary with those who make a contract." Thereupon, opening his Sacred Heart, he enclosed her right hand within it, solemnly promising to confirm in her all the graces he had given. When she withdrew her hand, she found that the fingers were encircled by seven gold rings in token of the privileges she had received. In an antiphon in honor of St. Gertrude this favor is recalled by the words, *annulis septem.* Later, however, it seemed to her that she had acted perversely in "demanding signs and wonders."

Remembering the many special favors she had received and wondering which of them would be of the greatest use to others, Gertrude was thus counseled by Christ: "The greatest advantage for men is to know that I, son of a virgin, stand always before God the Father to plead the cause of the human race. If they defile their hearts through human frailty I offer my Sacred Heart in reparation. If they sin with their mouths, I offer my innocent mouth for them. If they offend him by their actions, I offer my pierced hands for them. . . . I wish, therefore, that after they have so easily obtained forgiveness, they would thank me for it."

When fatigue prevented St. Gertrude from reciting the Little Hours of our Lady (not of obligation but often recited as an exercise of devotion by religious who are bound to say the Divine Office) she asked what service to the Blessed Virgin she might render instead. "Praise me," said Christ, "through my Heart for the innocence of her perfect virginity." The saint perceived that through her offering of the Sacred Heart, our Lady appeared to be most joyfully refreshed. She therefore replaced each hour of the Little Office with this offering, acknowledging each time some special grace received by Mary.

*　　*　　*

Even in her preparations for the feast of the Nativity,

St. Gertrude venerated the wounds of Christ. She concluded her exercise with an act of homage to the wound in his side, greeting the Sacred Heart with profound love and glorifying it as containing all the incomprehensible mysteries of the divinity. A few days after this feast, when she was learning from St. John of the graces he had received during the Last Supper, she was shown his state of beatitude in heaven—within the Sacred Heart there was an immense ocean, and in it the beloved apostle "like a fish" in perfect joy and freedom. (This comparison is frequently found in the literature of mysticism; it occurs several times in the *Dialogue* of St. Catherine of Siena.)

During the days of the Carnival before Lent, Gertrude was told by Christ to say the *Laudate Dominum* while offering to God all the weariness and labors of the Sacred Heart for the salvation of men.

When St. Gertrude prayed for others, Christ said to her: "You have enkindled in my Heart a flame of love for each of these persons." With her customary magnanimity the saint then asked how she could so inflame the Sacred Heart for every soul in the Church. "In four ways," he answered; "first, by praising me for having created all in my image; second, by thanking me for all the benefits I have already given them and those which I shall yet give; third, by sorrowing over the obstacles that they put in the way of my grace; fourth, by praying for all who, according to the plans of my providence, strive for perfection for the sake of my honor and glory."

The unceasing efficacy of the Sacred Heart for the salvation of the world was represented to St. Gertrude under the figure of its two pulsations: by one was accomplished the conversion of sinners; by the other, the sanctification of the just. And as no human activity, such as seeing, hearing, or working can interrupt the movement of man's heart, so the interceding pulsation of the Sacred Heart will continue undiminished until the end of time.

As Gertrude meditated on the coming of the Holy Spirit to the disciples, Christ said to her: "If you wish to receive him, you must touch my side and my hands as the disciples did." By these words she realized that to touch the side of Christ is to acknowledge with gratitude the love of the Sacred Heart for us, notwithstanding our ingratitude.

On the feast of Pentecost, Christ, as he had done before, opened his Sacred Heart to the saint, and as she knelt in adoration, enclosed her in it as a sign of her perfect union of will with him. On an earlier occasion he had said to her: "Your will is the key to your heart. Give it to me." Now to manifest her complete dedication to him, St. Gertrude presented her head, her hands, and finally her feet in order that her intentions, her desires, and all her actions might be sanctified.

More than once, the saint saw Christ gathering into his Heart various actions and prayers which pleased him; for example, on the feast of St. Bernard, he drew into his Heart all the merit and devotion won by anyone through the words and writings of the holy abbot. A similar honor was paid to St. Augustine on his feast day. On the Assumption, St. Gertrude saw the Blessed Virgin pouring into the Sacred Heart the perfume of her virtues which appeared as thornless roses, lilies, violets, and other flowers. On the feast of St. Ursula, Christ promised St. Gertrude that he would fill the lamp of her heart with grace from his own.

A number of the saint's revelations concerning the Sacred Heart took place on the feast of the Dedication of the Church. It was on this day that she was permitted to enter the Sacred Heart, which became for her a mansion of delights. "My Lord," she exclaimed, "it would have been enough for me to stand where your feet had stood, but

how can I thank you for this overwhelming privilege?"
Christ responded: "Since you often give me your noblest
possession, your heart, it is only just that you should find
your delight in mine: I am your God, all in all to you—
strength, life, knowledge, nourishment, clothing—all that
you can desire."

Realizing that all she had done was only owing to his
grace, Gertrude still felt the reward to be undeserved, but
Christ said: "It is my way to repay with blessings anyone
whom I have anticipated with my help; if he abandons
himself to me to fulfill the good pleasure of my Divine
Heart, I in my turn conform to his wishes."

It was through the Sacred Heart that St. Gertrude atoned
for negligence in the service of the Blessed Virgin. She appealed to Christ to enable her to offer his Mother the homage she deserved. Frequently after such prayers she saw
Christ glorifying and gladdening Mary with the treasures
of his Sacred Heart. One of the most beautiful of such
scenes occurred on the feast of the Assumption when St.
Gertrude offered to the Blessed Virgin the antiphon *Ista
pulchra est,* chanted at Vespers. As she did so, she saw a
shower of stars passing from the Sacred Heart to adorn
the Mother of God. They were so numerous that many
fell to the ground and the saints joyfully gathered them.
This was to signify that all the blessed share in the Queen
of Heaven's superabundant merits granted by the Heart of
her Son.

SUMMARY

It seems that all St. Gertrude's special graces were associated with the Sacred Heart. When she sought a con-
firmation of Christ's gifts to her, he opened with both
hands "the ark of divine love and infallible truth" and
from within it adorned her hand with seven rings testifying

to his fidelity. The gift of Christ's special friendship for her is summed up in the Sacred Heart, so that in recapitulating all that she has received, she says: ". . . You have admitted me to the incomparable intimacy of your love by opening to me the most noble ark of your divinity, that is to say, your Sacred Heart, that I might find my delight in it; you have freely given it to me, or you have exchanged it for mine as a manifest sign of your tender familiarity. By this divine Heart I have known your secret judgments. By it you have given me so many and such sweet proofs of your love that if I did not know your unspeakable condescension, I should be astonished to see you lavish them even upon your Blessed Mother although she is the most excellent of creatures and reigns with you in heaven."

All three of the mystics of Helfta had certainly assimilated the patristic, objective attitude toward the Sacred Heart as described at the beginning of this chapter. Their personal relations with the Savior did not supersede, but rather reinforced the traditional veneration.

In their astonishing familiarity with the Sacred Heart, nevertheless, each of the three mystics of Helfta manifests an individual emphasis. Mechtild von Magdeburg has been called "the poet of a sanctified, transfigured, glorified sorrow, most acceptable offering to the divine Heart of Jesus."[6] St. Mechtild von Hackeborn, on the other hand, is captivated by the glorified Heart of the triumphant Christ. For St. Gertrude, the association of the Passion and the Holy Eucharist with the Sacred Heart inspires a multitude of images, striking in their range and richness. At various times she perceives it under the aspect of a lyre or harp played on by the Holy Spirit; as an organ, source of delight for the Trinity; as a chalice from which

[6] Eric Colledge, "Mechtild of Magdeburg" *The Month* CCXI (June, 1961) 335.

the elect drink; as a censer through which the prayers of the faithful mount to God in fragrance; as a burning lamp; a treasure-house of the divinity; a golden altar; a portal of salvation; a stream flowing with honey; a marvelous palace.

More notable, however, is the exalted love and noble confidence of Gertrude's intercourse with the Heart of Christ perceived as an immediate presence. It is this that forms the atmosphere of her *Legatus Divinae Pietatis*, making it truly "the messenger of God's loving kindness," a central document in the theological and devotional literature of the Sacred Heart.

The Death of Gertrude

It is in the death of St. Gertrude that her union with the Sacred Heart is most apparent. One of the proofs of the genuineness of mystical union is that the privileged person desires to be dissolved and to be with Christ. According to one authority, "True union can always be identified by the soul's ardent longings for death, if it should be with the will of God, and meanwhile, the desire to suffer, to work, and to endure reproaches for his sake without any regard for human considerations."[1]

Both of these desires are to be found in St. Gertrude. When she wished to recover her health in order to follow the rule more exactly, she was rebuked by Christ for opposing his will. "But my only desire is for your glory!" she protested. "I regard your prayer as a child's," he answered. "If you were to insist further, I should not be pleased." At other times when she longed to die, Gertrude was taught that such longing should be united to perfect submission to God's will. One who, while desiring death, yet was content to live as long as Providence ordained, would receive in recompense all the merits of the most holy life of the Son of God.

[1] Arintero, *Mystical Evolution*, II, 162.

Having learned this lesson of tranquil resignation to the will of Christ, Gertrude expressed it in one of her most attractive comparisons: "When a bridegroom conducts his bride into a garden of roses to gather them for a bouquet, she takes so much pleasure in his conversation that she never pauses to inquire which of the roses he wishes her to gather, but she takes whichever flower her bridegroom gives her and places it in her bouquet. So also the faithful soul. . . ."

HER PREPARATIONS

Gertrude's many illnesses and the deaths of her fellow-religious kept constantly in her mind the importance of a good preparation for eternity. Accordingly, she was accustomed to perform a number of special devotions with this intention. Every Friday at noon she withdrew to say for herself the prayers for those in their agony. After she had done so for some time she was granted a consoling revelation of her own death in which she saw herself in the arms of Christ, her head supported by the Blessed Virgin, while an immense number of angels and saints sang the *Salve Regina.* They held censers from which issued the prayers of the entire Church. Her guardian angel under the aspect of a noble prince rejoiced at the happiness soon to be hers. The demons, who had the appearance of hideous toads and serpents were so powerless that the angels did not even drive them away; they vanished of their own accord at the sight of a column of fire mounting from the dying saint to the throne of God.

Moreover, as each saint was invoked in the litany, he came forth to assist her. A rich, pageant-like effect was created by the description of these celestial allies, each with his appropriate symbol: the patriarchs carried branches from which hung fruits representing their good works; the prophets had golden mirrors depicting their revelations; the martyrs, palms; the confessors, golden flowers; the virgins, roses; the widows, golden caskets. Gertrude's special friend, St. John the Evangelist, offered her two golden rings. The other apostles also gave her rings to signify their fidelity to Christ. All of these gifts indicated that the saints were sharing their merits with her.

Finally, the Son of the Most High, the King of Glory, inclining himself, drew Gertrude into eternal life "as a dewdrop is absorbed by the sun." The Solesmes editors note that this is a mystical exposition, although it is given as an historical account. The entire fifth book of the *Legatus* is, in fact, such an exposition; the writer, Gertrude's unknown friend, has in only a few passages given any information about the external circumstances of the saint's death.

We do know, however, that in addition to her weekly preparation, Gertrude used to make a five-day retreat every year with the intention of obtaining the grace of a good death. (St. Mechtild also made it a practice to follow these exercises.) As her illness became more serious Gertrude redoubled the fervor of her preparations, uniting all her actions to those of Christ that they might be sanctified by his innocence and be performed only for him.

One of the most striking manifestations of the Sacred Heart occurred during these last days of her life. At the elevation of the mass, Christ opened his Heart with both hands. Flames came forth from it and fused her heart with his. From the two hearts a tree of gold and silver sprang up, shining like the sun. "This tree has grown from the union of your will with mine," said Christ. The branches were hung with magnificent fruits which bowed down over all those for whom the saint had prayed.

"Is this illness taking me to you?" she asked of the Savior. "It brings you nearer to me," he answered.

On the feast of St. Martin, November 11, Gertrude felt an intense desire to die when she read the response: "Blessed Martin knew the hour of his death long beforehand." "When will you grant me the same news, O Lord?" she asked. "Soon," he replied. During the next Easter week the same conversation was repeated, and Christ added, "During the time that remains to you, do not live for yourself but for my glory."

At a later time he said, "Choose whichever you wish—either to die forthwith or to have the merit of a long illness though you fear that thereby you may add to the number of your faults." He was pleased when she left the choice entirely to him. "If for my love you consent to live here longer, I shall dwell in you and you in me like a dove in the rocks until I lead you into the land of eternal spring." After that time, whenever Gertrude grew impatient for death, Christ said to her: "What true bride would desire to reach the place where her spouse can no longer add to her adornment nor she prepare gifts for him?"

AN ALLEGORICAL DIALOGUE

An allegorical dialogue which gives a most attractive impression of the saint's familiarity with Christ has to do with his promise to provide her with a spiritual conveyance at the time of her departure from this life. Two angels were to sound the trumpet to announce the tidings: "Behold the bridegroom cometh. Go forth to meet him." She asked eagerly: "What will be the chariot?" "My divine desire," was the answer. "Where shall I be seated?" "Your confidence in my goodness will be the seat." "And the reins?" "Fervent love." "Lord," she suddenly exclaimed, "you know that I don't understand what other things are necessary for an equipage! I don't know what else to ask." Christ answered, "No matter what you were to ask, I promise that your joys will go beyond all that you could see or imagine. The human mind cannot conceive what I have prepared for my chosen ones, and this inability is my delight."

At one time, St. Gertrude expressed a desire to die in the church where she had received the mystical wound of love, but Christ said to her: "When your soul goes forth from this world, I shall place you under the shadow of my fatherly protection and with motherly care carry and cover you as a woman protects her beloved infant when she is crossing a stormy sea. When the journey is over, I shall fill you with unspeakable joys in heaven, just as the mother does not mean merely to save her child from the sea, but to bring him to shore." Thereupon the saint abandoned herself to God's will to determine the place as well as the time of her death.

It seemed to her that at an earlier date she had been better prepared to die, but since then had become negligent because of Christ's delay in calling her. "All things have their time according to my wise providence," she was told. "I have faithfully kept for you whatever you have already done, and nothing that you add thereto will be lost." From this she learned that one may prepare for death long in advance, just as a prince may store wine and grain in his cellar to make ready for his marriage.

HELP OF SINNERS

Gertrude was habitually conscious of her membership in the universal Church and never more so than in her last days on earth. She praised God for the graces, gifts, and glory bestowed on the Blessed Virgin, and for the merits and joys of all the saints and angels. One of Christ's promises to her was that on the day of her death he would for her sake draw to himself carnal and earthly souls. She was also assured that those who assisted her in her last illness would be richly rewarded; that many souls would be released from Purgatory and enter heaven with her; that those who prayed for her or thanked God for his goodness to her should receive most abundant graces and favors.

Years before, Gertrude had learned that "adversity is the spiritual ring that espouses the soul to Christ." Now in her last sufferings it was in union with his Passion that she prepared herself for eternal life. The Sacred Heart became for her the source of strength, peace, and sweetness, changing her sufferings into joy. Meditating on her obligations as a religious and her imperfect performance of her duties, she said prayers of reparation, particularly for her negligence in the recitation of the office. She also avowed her faults against her neighbors—specifically, want of consideration, failure to give thanks, rejoice, or grieve with them. She reread her rule, endeavoring to atone for her failure to observe it, and for failing to offer praise, thanksgiving, supplication, and reparation for the whole Church. The consolation that she received in return was so great that the nuns desired to be near her in order to hear her instructions, and they said many prayers that her life might be prolonged.

Among the prayers that she most often repeated were the lines from the *Jesu Dulcis Memoria:*

> Desiderate millies,
> Mi Jesu, quando venies?
> Me laetum quando facies?
> De te me quando saties?
> Veni, veni, Rex optime!
> Pater immensae gloriae,
> Effulge clare laetius,
> Jam exspectamus saepius.

As she had so often done, she once more grieved for her insufficient devotion to the Blessed Virgin, and once again Christ, "the King of Glory, offered his Divine Heart to his Mother, asking her to assist Gertrude as a true mother at the hour of her death."

St. Gertrude died in 1301 or 1302. Although her sisters had said, "When she dies, she should be put under our altar with the relics of the saints," she was probably buried in the convent cemetery, but the actual site of her grave is not known.

THE CULT OF GERTRUDE

Strange to say, despite her reputation for holiness and the approval of her writings by several theologians, St. Gertrude unlike St. Mechtild, did not attract general interest immediately after her death. As has been noted earlier, her *Legatus* survives in only a few manuscripts, and it was not until the invention of printing that her work became known. With the edition of Lanspergius in 1536, the name of Gertrude began to be illustrious. Spain was one of the first countries to have the *Legatus* in the vernacular, and as Ledos says, the translation appeared "crowned with the approbation of the most renowned theologians: Diego Yepes, S.J. and Domingo Bañez, O.P. [both confessors of St. Teresa]; Francisco Suarez, S.J.; and other religious, Carmelites, Franciscans, and Benedictines."[2]

The first official evidence of a cult dates from October 7, 1606, when the Apostolic See gave permission to the nuns of St. John the Evangelist in Licenza to recite an office in honor of St. Gertrude. The association of St. Gertrude and St. John in the devotion to the Sacred Heart gives significance to this event. Three years later a similar

[2] Gabriel Ledos, *Sainte Gertrude* (Paris, 1903) p. 203.

favor was given to a community in Mexico, the nuns of the Conception of the Blessed Virgin. In 1654, the Benedictine monks and nuns of the Congregation of Monte Cassino, and soon thereafter all Benedictine congregations, were allowed to say the Office of St. Gertrude.

THE FEAST OF ST. GERTRUDE

Although never formally canonized, Gertrude was nevertheless included in the Roman Martyrology in 1677. After a careful inquiry the following entry was made: *"17 Novembris in Germania, S. Gertrudis Virginis Ordinis S. Benedicti, quae dono revelationum clara exstitit."* In the next century the kingdom of Poland and the Duchy of Saxony were accorded the privilege of a mass and office in honor of the saint. On July 20, 1738, her feast was extended to the entire Church.

The Office of St. Gertrude commemorates her humility, her devotion to the Eucharist and the Passion, and her stigmata. The line, *"Adjuvabat eam Deus vultu suo,"* alludes to her vision of the face of Christ. One of the responsories perpetuates the words often inscribed on her portrait: *"In corde Gertrudis invenietis me."*

St. Gertrude's feast has been celebrated variously on November 15, 16, and 17. When she was to be assigned a day in the Roman Calendar, November 17 was at first proposed. That day, however, was already assigned to St. Gregory the Wonderworker. The Pontiff, Clement XII, was of the opinion that a saint who had moved mountains should not himself be moved; it was moreover improper, he declared, that a bishop and doctor should yield his place to a virgin! Since neither the exact date nor year of Gertrude's death was given in the *Legatus* (it is said only that she died shortly after the feast of St. Lebuin, which is on November 12) it was decided that her feast would be assigned to November 15. At present, the Roman Calendar lists it on November 16; some communities of Benedictines, however, keep it on the following day, St. Gregory Thaumaturgus notwithstanding.

Among her other honors, St. Gertrude has been declared patroness of the Indies. In New Mexico, her feast is celebrated with great solemnity. Her title, "la magna," was given to her by Prosper Cardinal Lambertini, later Benedict XIV, in his treatise entitled *De servorum Dei beatificatione.*

GERTRUDE'S INFLUENCE

Engelbert Krebs asserts that through her devotion to the Sacred Heart, St. Gertrude has a strong influence on the French "baroque mysticism" of the seventeenth and eighteenth centuries.[3] Of St. Margaret Mary and Blessed Claude de la Colombière, the two seventeenth-century apostles of the Sacred Heart, it is said that Christ's revelations to them "only amplified and confirmed what he had long before taught St. Gertrude." Gertrude's mission is summed up in the title of her book, *Legatus Divinae Pietatis, The Herald of the Divine Loving-Kindness.* The book was written in fulfillment of her special vocation; that much of it was dictated assured at least some dissemination of her teachings.

Ledos has made penetrating comments on St. Gertrude's role, pointing out that even she did not at first understand it—hence her difficulty in submitting to Christ's command that she write.[4] He did not give the order in his own person only, but also through her superiors and companions. Gertrude's gradual realization that she must share God's

[3] "Gertrude v. Helfta" in *Die Deutsche Literatur des Mittelalters Verfasserlexikon,* ed. Wolfgang Stammler (Berlin, 1936) II, 44.
[4] Ledos, p. 164.

gifts had the twofold effect of making her docile to the divine inspiration and humble in recognizing that she was appointed to assist others. "Alas!" she said, "by my useless words I have wasted the talent thou didst so liberally bestow on me. But now I may gain some merit by what I share with others." It was largely through the admonitions of St. Mechtild that St. Gertrude began to understand her obligation to disclose her knowledge of the love and mercy of God.

When Gertrude complained to Christ that she had a thousand desires that she could not fulfill because of her health and circumstances, he gave her the reason for these apparently incompatible aspirations: "I have done this so that in your book each will find what he needs to console and instruct him." (St. Gertrude's experience reminds one of St. Thérèse of Lisieux who exclaimed, "I feel called to the priesthood and to the apostolate—I would be a martyr, a doctor of the Church. . . . One mission alone would not satisfy my longings.")

Every one of Gertrude's special opportunities—her secular studies, her familiarity with the works of the Fathers of the Church, her conversations with her friends—served to complement her spiritual progress and, as it were, to form her as an effective instrument for spreading the great doctrine of the Sacred Heart, its universal and infinite love and mercy.

More than six centuries ago, St. Gertrude realized with incredulous love how greatly Christ wished to dwell within her. In selfless impetuosity she had responded to her Lord with all the energy of her keen intellect and ardent personality. It is this that the Church singles out today above all of St. Gertrude's graces for commemoration in the prayer offered during the mass in her honor:

"O God, who didst prepare for thyself a pleasant abode

in the heart of thy holy virgin Gertrude, let her merits and pleading move thee to wash away the sins by which our hearts are stained and grant us fellowship with her in bliss."

No saint needs a shrine, but the friends of a saint find joy in visiting the places he has made holy. For Gertrude's friends her writings are her imperishable memorial. There we see and hear her, exalted to the heights of contemplation yet endearingly natural: falling asleep at mass and being awakened by the bell at the consecration; taking to her bed "to escape the tumult of visitors"; quixotically wishing to die that she might set God free from the debt of mercy which his love obliged him to contract for her salvation. We find her subject to the ordinary experiences of a conventual household: listening to the bell that calls the workmen to their meals; noting that "some persons frightened by nightmares cry out in a fearful manner"; receiving her portion of food and clothing as if from the hand of God. We see also the panorama of life at Helfta: the great-hearted Abbess Gertrude von Hackeborn, the gentle and ardent St. Mechtild her sister, the storm-beaten yet fiery Mechtild von Magdeburg, and a host of others, among them Gertrude's friend, the unnamed *"compila-trix,"*—"another learned virgin," as Lanspergius calls her. Yet beloved and companioned as St. Gertrude was, our final image of her is a solitary figure, transfixed in love and adoration of the Sacred Heart. "I am your closest relative," Christ said to her, *"ego propinquissimus sum*—your father, your brother, your spouse."

"Fellowship with her in bliss," we ask in her mass. But we hear the words of the Lord to Moses, "Take off the shoes from thy feet: thou art on holy ground," as we follow St. Gertrude into the Land of Likeness.

213